Encounters with the Light
Two novelettes on real encounters with the Imam of the Time (a.) by **Elāheh Beheshtī**

The Fourteenth Tale (p 7),
and
The Mystery of the Miraculous Pomegranate (p 73)

Rendered into English and Annotated by
Blake Archer Williams

Originally published under the titles
سرود سرخ انار and و آن که دیرتر آمد
Copyright © 2016 by Jamkaran Publications, Qom, Iran
Copyright in English © 2025 by Lantern Publications

All rights reserved. No part of this publication may be reproduced, distributed, or transmitted in any form or by any means, including photocopying, recording, or other electronic or mechanical methods, without the prior written permission of the publisher, except in the case of brief quotations embodied in critical reviews and certain other noncommercial uses permitted by copyright law. For permission requests, write to the publisher, addressed "Attention: - Permissions (Encounters with the Light)," at the email address below.

Lantern Publications
info@lanternpublications.com
www.lanternpublications.com

Ordering Information:
Quantity sales. Special discounts are available on quantity purchases by corporations, associations, and others. For details, contact the distributor at the address below.

Shia Books Australia
www.shiabooks.com.au
info@shiabooks.com.au

ISBN- 978-1-922583-73-4(PBK)

In the Name of God,
The Most Compassionate, the Most Merciful

Prayers of God's Peace and Blessings

In keeping with the Islamic practice of showing respect for the name of God, and sending prayers of God's peace and blessings whenever the name of His blessed Prophet, Lady Fāṭimah, and the Twelve Imams is mentioned, as well as for asking God to hasten the reappearance of the Lord of the Age on the Earthly plane, one or more of the following Arabic symbols have been employed throughout the text. They are repeated for their great rewards.

 Used exclusively after the name of God, meaning "the Sublimely Exalted," or, as a prayer, "[May His name be] Sublimely Exalted".

 Used exclusively after the name of the Prophet, meaning "May the peace and blessings of God be unto him and unto [the purified and inerrant members of] his family"

 Used for any of the Twelve Imams or past prophets of God, meaning "May God's peace be unto him".

 Used for two or more of the Twelve Imams or past prophets of God, meaning "May God's peace be unto them".

 Used for Lady Fāṭimah, meaning "May God's peace be unto her".

 Used for a plurality of the Fourteen Immaculates, meaning "May God's peace be unto them all collectively".

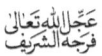 Used for the Master of the Age (the Twelfth Imam), meaning "May God hasten his sacred reappearance".

The Fourteenth Tale

1

My name is Mīrzā Ḥusain, and I'm a writer and a scribe. I was afflicted by a terrible illness fourteen months ago, which could not be cured by any of the doctors that I called on. I sought refuge with the Imams ﷺ, vowing that if I were to be cured of my illness, I would write a story for each of the Fourteen Infallibles ﷺ in the next fourteen months, taking a month to write a story about each of them in turn. After I was cured, I was able to write thirteen of the fourteen stories that I had vowed to write, but I was unable to find a story that was worthy of the Twelfth Imam ﷺ, and as the days passed, I had become despondent as to how I was going to be able to fulfil my sacred vow (*nadhr*).

This situation continued until only one day remained before the deadline of my *nadhr*, at which point I was invited to a gathering. I really didn't feel like going because being in the company of others prevented me from being fretful and feeling sorry for myself. But what is strange is that when I got there, I heard a wonderous tale about an incident that had occurred to a man who was known as Mahmoud the Persian. There were differences of opinion about the details of the incident, but I could not contain my joy at finally having found the fourteenth tale! I resolved to find Mahmoud the Persian that same day and to hear the story from himself at first-hand, especially as I had been told that he lived in my own town, in a neighbourhood that was not far from my house.

I had heard Mahmoud the Persian's story from a fellow named Muslim on whom I eventually prevailed to take me to Mahmoud's house. Muslim kept telling me to leave it for another day, and that we were guests there [at the party], and so on. He even said that his legs were weak! I insisted that tomorrow would be too late, and that I would not be able to fulfil my *nadhr*. Anyway, he finally relented, and we took off. He was telling the truth; he was an old man whose mind was still sharp, but his legs were indeed feeble. He ambulated slowly and stopped at every opportunity he got to exchange pleasantries with passersby.

I ran out of patience and asked, "Is there much longer to go?"

He shook his head and said, 'No, just a couple more streets.

The Fourteenth Tale

I asked, 'Can't you tell me where his house is so that I can go on ahead of you?'

He smiled and said, 'Either I walk very slowly, or you have become very impatient.' He then used his cane to point to the end of the alley and said, 'It's at the end of the alley, in the cul-de-sac.'

I picked up my pace and turned into the long cul-de-sac, which I went to the end of. I wish I had asked which house it was, as there was more than one. I waited impatiently until Muslim finally showed up at the mouth of the cul-de-sac. He walked a little way, then stood in front of the door of one of the houses in the cul-de-sac. Then, he let me know with a shake of his head and a motion of his arm that I had gone too far. By the time I reached him, Muslim had already knocked on the door.

A boy opened the door, and a smile broke out on his face as soon as he saw it was Muslim. He offered his *salām* (a greeting of peace) and stepped aside from the door opening to make way for us to enter. After we had entered, I took hold of Muslim's arm and whispered in his ear, "It didn't occur to me that it might have been impolite of us to make an unannounced visit like this."

Muslim said, 'Don't worry. Mahmoud's door is always open to the Shī'a of Imam Ali ﷺ.'

He then reached into the pocket of his *abā* (cloak) and gave the boy a fistful of raisins and dried dates. We were led into a small room, which was plain but clean. A man dressed in a white cassock who had black hair and wore a black beard was seated in the room, reading the Quran. When we offered him our *salāms*, he raised his head from the book and looked at us with a pair of blue eyes that sparkled brilliantly. When he saw Muslim, a smile came to his face, and he made a motion to stand up.

I said, "Please, there is no need for you to get up." I then went and placed my hand on his shoulder to prevent him from offering us that courtesy. But he rose up, despite the pressure my hand was applying to his shoulder. I thought to myself, what a well-mannered man he is. I said, "You are too kind."

He replied, "Not at all! What can be a better pleasure than beholding the visage of a couple of true believers?"

After we had kissed each other's cheeks three times, as is our custom after the example of our Prophet ﷺ and Imams ﷺ, he said in a low voice, "Especially if they have the scent of Heaven about them."

His words and appearance made a good impression on me. After he and I had exchanged kisses on each other's cheeks, we sat down. Mahmoud's brilliant and penetrating eyes prevented me from being able to speak while looking directly into his eyes.

Muslim straightened up a little and said, 'We were at a gathering and your name came up, together with that story of what happened to you. This gentleman is eager to hear the story in your own words. His name is Mīrzā Ḥusain, the Scribe, and it seems he has made a sacred vow to write down ḥadīth reports

The Fourteenth Tale

about our Imams ﷺ. And so, if you are so inclined, be as kind as to relate the tale to him.'

Mahmoud let out a deep sigh and said, "My dear friend! You know full well that I do not tell this tale to anyone who just happens to want to hear it, especially if that person is a stranger. There are untrustworthy ears about who not only will not be affected by the retelling of the tale, but who might cause problems to arise."

I said, "I am not a stranger, my brother. I am one of the faithful ones and am anxious to hear about your adventure." And then I added in a jocular vein, "If you don't tell me your story, I will sit here until you do."

Muslim also came to my aid, adding, "It might be that this is a part of God's ﷻ plan and that our friend here will be the means to doing some good. What he says and writes might cause some souls to be guided aright!"

Without saying another word, Mahmoud took up the Qur'ān, sat facing the *Qibla* (or the Muslim direction of prayer, facing the Ka'ba in Mecca), and opened the book as a way of performing a divination (*istikhāra*). As fate would have it, the divination turned out to be positive.

Mahmoud said, "I will relate this tale in my own words, using my own idioms, but it will be up to you to do justice to the story with the power of your quill."

I nodded slowly and deeply but said nothing, and after a long pause, Mahmoud continued, "But I have one condition, and that is that the truth must not be violated in any way."

"Unquestionably! On my word of honour, sire," I replied.

I quickly took out my quill, inkpot, my slate tablet and some paper, and was ready to listen and to take notes. When Mahmoud the Persian observed my excitement, he smiled and began to tell his tale; and this is what he said.

2

I was born in a village near Hilla, whose inhabitants are Sunni. I spent my teenage years there. The village was separated from Hilla and the rest of the world by a barren desert. One of the pastimes of the village's youth was to be on the lookout for caravans that were passing through, in the hope of getting a small reward for giving the glad tidings to the people of the caravan that they were close to arriving at our village.

I don't remember who it was that gave me the news that day, that a large caravan would be arriving at the village by noon. I immediately went to see Ahmad upon hearing the news, and didn't tell anyone else about it. Ahmad clapped his hands with pleasure and said, "Great! If the caravan is as large as you say it is, we'll be sure to get a few coins out of it. Let's go and tell the other kids."

"Forget that!" I said, "Why spend all the time going and finding everyone else when we can keep all of the coins to ourselves?"

I eventually prevailed on him to forego telling everyone else. There was still a lot of time left before the sun reached its peak when we set out from our village, and because we thought it would not be long before we reached the caravan, we didn't think we needed to take any water or provisions with us. We walked for hours and put a large swath of the desert behind us, without getting any sight of a dust cloud that a large caravan would create in its wake. The sun was now high up in the middle of the sky, and its heat burned our heads. Ahmad came to a stop, dried his forehead with a corner of his *keffiyeh*, and said, "Are you sure you heard right?"

"I heard it with my own ears."

I wiped the sweat of my brow with my sleeve, cursing myself for not having taken my *keffiyeh*. Ahmad shaded his eyes with his hand, scanned the horizon and said, "Well, then where is it?! Do you see anything but sand?"

I pointed at the farthest sand dune and said, "Let's go up to that point, and head back if we don't see anything by then."

The Fourteenth Tale

He put his hands on his hips and said with a frown, "Head back? Just like that? We've come all this way just to go back empty-handed?"

I just shrugged and started walking again, because I knew that whatever else he would say would just irritate me more. Ahmad followed, grumbling, "No water... No food... Because you were in such a hurry!"

It took every ounce of our strength for us to finally reach the top of the sand dune. It was a little past noon, and the heat was truly oppressive. I could see how Ahmad had started to drag his feet from fatigue and thirst. The sun had burned his face, and he was panting, nor was I in any better shape. I was completely parched. The hot grains of sand that made their way through the laces of my shoes burned my feet. My head was burning up as I had not thought of bringing anything to protect it against the blazing sun. My eyes were also blacking out from time to time. When we finally made it up the dune with great difficulty, we saw nothing but an endless expanse of desert; there was no dust-trail of any caravan, no oasis, and not even a single palm tree.

Ahmad let out a groan and sat down. He took off his shoes and shook the hot sand out of them.

I said, 'Get up. You'll burn yourself.'

He just shook his head and said, 'So much for you and your "news" of a caravan.'

I said, 'How is it my fault? I just repeated what I heard.'

The Fourteenth Tale

I was so tired that I eventually sat down too. I yelled out when the heat of the sand coursed through my whole body and hit my head like a shock wave.

Ahmad said, 'Serves you right! Whatever we have suffered is all on account of your thoughtlessness.' He then threw a fistful of sand at me.

I said, 'What was *that* for? You are the one who said this is the way we should come!' And then, just out of spite, I added, 'The rest of the guys have probably met up with the caravan already and gotten a good reward.'

'Now you're getting sassy too? I'll show you "a good reward".'

And before I could move, he had jumped up and was on top of me. Ahmad was bigger and stronger than I was, so before he could grab hold of me, I placed my knee on his chest and shoved him to my right. But before I had thrown him off me, Ahmad had grabbed a hold of my collar, and as a result, we both rolled down the sand dune with the momentum of his fall. I don't know what I hit my head on, but before I knew it, I felt everything whirling around me, and then I passed out.

When I came to, it felt like I had been gently shaken awake. Then I felt like I was perhaps being swayed back and forth on the soft-cushioned litter or palanquin of a camel that treaded lightly through the sands. Gradually, I came to my senses. The palanquin of the camel turned out to be Ahmad's shoulders, on which he was carrying me. He had wrapped his keffiyeh around my head and neck. He was panting heavily, and the back of his neck was wet with his sweat. The sun blazed down on us as we made our way through the bleak desert. The Devil tempted me to stay still so that I could continue to be carried on the back of those soft shoulders. The prospect of the scorching sand and what it would do to my feet was sufficient enticement for me to give in to the Devil's temptation. Our shadow followed us like a strange but steadfast animal. When I saw Ahmad's shadow, I felt sorry for him, and my heart went out to him. He was doubled over in pain and was dragging his feet on the hot sand. I felt so ashamed of myself. I made a move to dismount, and as soon as I did that, Ahmad immediately relieved himself of the heavy burden of my load and bent over, looking at me. His face was sunburned, and his lips were dry and chapped. He made a swallowing gesture with difficulty, then asked, 'Are you ok?'

I nodded my affirmation.

He smiled and said, 'Is everything ok?'

He said it in such a way that I really felt sorry for him. I had no idea how long he had been carrying me, but what was important to me was the righteousness of character that he had clearly demonstrated. I moved his keffiyeh aside, embraced him lovingly, and said, 'Forgive me.'

I lay down on my back. My tongue was as dry as a piece of kindling.

Ahmad said, 'Hang in there.'

Death was staring me in the face. The image of my mother's tears and my father's grief appeared before my eyes. The question occurred to me as to whether or not they would even find my dead body. Suddenly, a great shiver of fear ran through my body. What if they don't find my corpse? I thought of the wolves of the desert and how we would be eaten alive by them if they were to come across us before we died. The thought was so terrifying that I grabbed hold of Ahmad's hand involuntarily. The look in my eye betrayed what was going through my mind.

'I hope that we will die sooner rather than later,' I said, giving expression to my fear.

He bit his lip, and it was not long before I saw tears run down his cheeks. He placed both his hands on his cheeks and said in a choked-up voice, 'Let us make a *tawassul*.'[1]

I said, '*Tawassul*? It's useless. We're done for.' I let out a deep groan and slapped my head with both hands.

Ahmad said, 'Don't give way to despair. God is "the Most Merciful". He responds to the pleas of his faithful servants.'

He was right. And in any event, it was better than doing nothing. I said, 'O Lord! ...'

---

[1] *Tawassul*: Intercessory recourse. *Tawassul* is a specific type of intercessory recourse in which someone resorts to or takes recourse in various instruments that have been made available to him by God ﷻ (such as to supplications or to the spirit of a prophet, Imam, or saint) as *an intermediary means for help* in his endeavors to recommend himself to the notice, favor, or mercy of God ﷻ.

The Fourteenth Tale

My eyelids drooped in exhaustion, and I closed my eyes and thought that if Ahmad's pleas reached God's ﷻ ears and He willed to save him, Ahmad would be saved, and I would be saved along with him.

Ahmad supplicated through his tears, 'O Lord! O Creator of the Heavens and of the Earth. I beseech you on the right of the dignity and honour (*izza^t*) of Your Apostle ﷺ to save us from this situation that we are in.'

He mentioned the name of the Apostle of God ﷺ with such passion that it tore at my soul and caused a lump to form in my throat. I thought, 'Is it really possible for this plaintive plea to reach God's ﷻ Throne, and for Him to answer our plea?'

Ahmad's supplications eventually ended. I was looking at the sun, which was shivering like a mirage, blazing its blinding rays on us. Would that the sun would set sooner, so that we could at least die in the cooler night. This was to be the last sunset we would see in our short lives, which amounted to no more than thirteen years. It occurred to me that had I been a better person and had had a greater measure of faith, perhaps the Lord might have helped me. I was upset with myself, but also at my family, and especially at my father, who, while he was ostensibly an upright and staunch Muslim of one of the four Sunni rites, had fallen short in his duties of instilling in me the teachings of our religion. Whenever I would tell him that I had not learned how to perform the ritual devotions perfectly, he would say, 'Alright, we'll get to that later,' or some such remark. And so, I naturally thought, in my despondency, that I had given no thought to God ﷻ, so how could I expect Him to think of me now?

With the voice of my heart, I kept repeating, 'Forgive me, Lord. Forgive me...'

Suddenly, I saw two figures on top of a dune in the far distance. I squinted my eyes and focused. Sure enough, this was not a mirage! Two dark figures were coming towards us. I closed my eyes tightly and tried to gather my thoughts. Then I opened my eyes and looked again. No, this was definitely not a mirage! They had not disappeared. Not only had they not disappeared, but they could now be seen clearly, and the closer they came, the larger their figures grew. I thought of telling Ahmad immediately, for if he had seen them too, they would definitely be real, and we would have been saved. I called out to Ahmad, but my throat was so dry that nothing came out of my mouth. Ahmad might have passed out. I tried to grab his arm when I suddenly froze in fright.

A large black snake was slowly slithering up Ahmad's leg. I tried to move it, but couldn't. I could see him out of the corner of my eye, but I was so terrified that I couldn't even turn towards him. I let out a moan and pounded the sand with my fist, but Ahmad didn't move. The snake had made its way up to his chest by now. It took every ounce of my effort to reach out and touch the tips of Ahmad's fingers. He made a slight movement and opened his eyes. It was at this precise

The Fourteenth Tale

moment that the snake raised his head. It was preparing to strike Ahmad's face and neck and inject him with its venom. Ahmad let out a groan and was frozen stiff, petrified. But then, a shadow fell on Ahmad's chest. The snake turned towards the source of the shadow, after which it lowered its head and slowly made its way off Ahmad's chest and slithered away into the distance. It was as if it had been struck by a blow. I let out the breath that I was holding in my chest in a great sigh of relief. Ahmad's eyes were closed, and large beads of sweat had formed on his face. I squeezed his fingers, and it was only after I had done this that I became aware of the shadow of the riders who were seated on their horses above us.

One of them was dressed in white and was riding a white horse, and the other was a broad-shouldered man dressed in green and was riding a sorrel, holding a lance in his right hand. The two riders dismounted, and the rider dressed in white spread a throw rug within a few feet of us. The other man placed the tail end of his *amāmah* (turban) over his shoulders and sat facing us. I blacked out for an instant. I squeezed my face with my arm to help me regain my senses, and then heard Ahmad whispering, 'We've been saved.'

I raised my head with some difficulty. The man in white was middle-aged and lean, with greying hair and a grey beard. He had a light complexion and was standing behind the young man who was sitting in front of us and smiling. The young man's teeth were as white as pearls. He said in a resonant voice, 'What a ruckus you raised! The desert and the Heavens were set a-quiver with your "O Lords" and "O Apostle of Gods"!'

Ahmad said, 'Our voices weren't so loud.'

The young man said, 'They were loud enough, and they were passionate too.'

I thought to myself, 'How loud could our voices have *been* for them to have been heard at such a distance?!'

The young man pointed at Ahmad and said, 'Come over to me, Ahmad, the son of Yāsir.'

Ahmad stammered, 'Ye... yes... s... sir!' And he struck himself on the head and said in a lowered voice, 'This must be the Angel of Death, if he knows my name.'

My eyes opened wide out of fear and anxiety. I asked, 'How's that?'

Then I remembered how that viper fled from the rider, and so I pleaded to him, 'Don't leave us.'

The man smiled and said, 'Don't worry. You will only see good from me, not evil. Now get up and come over.'

Ahmad said, 'I can't. I don't have the strength.'

I don't know whether it was from fear or exhaustion that he was sprawled on the desert floor the way he was and couldn't move. The man said, 'You can. Now come over. You have grown up and are a man in your own right now.'

His voice was so soothing and pleasant to hear that if he had called me and asked for my life, I would

The Fourteenth Tale

have given it up to him. Ahmad crawled towards him. The young man ran his hand over Ahmad's head, then felt his bicep and back, then said, 'Now sit up.'

Ahmad slowly straightened himself up and sat kneeling before him. He straightened his shoulders and straightened out of his slouch. That's when my fear left me. What kind of Angel of Death was this who gives life rather than taking it away? Just as the thought of *'What about me'* was passing through my mind, the man turned to me and called out my name, 'Mahmoud!' and indicated with his hand that I too should approach. I made my way towards him on my hands and knees. He brought his hand forward, and I closed my eyes so that I could feel the caress of his hand on my head, shoulders, and arms. It felt as if a wave was coursing through my body, filling me with incredible power. As I felt this, I also smelled a scent so pleasant that I wanted nothing more than to stay there for days and nights on end, to feel the sense of his caress and smell the pleasantness of his scent. He gave a gentle tug at my earlobe and said, 'Now sit up.'

So, I sat kneeling before him and stared at him with eyes that had been charged with an incredible power I had not felt before. He was fair-skinned, and his cheeks had a little pink. He had a high forehead, and his hair and beard were jet black, which contrasted prominently with his fair skin. His eyebrows were slightly joined in the middle, and his deep brown eyes were so awe-inspiring, but it was impossible to stare at them for too long; it was also impossible *not* to stare at

The Fourteenth Tale

them! Ahmad was enamoured by him too and was staring at him.

The man said, 'Mahmoud, go and fetch a couple of bitter apples (*hanẓal*).²'

I got up and brought them to him. The young man turned one of the bitter apples around in his hand and then split it in two with his fingers. He held out one half to me and said, 'Eat it.'

Everyone knows how foul and bitter, bitter apples are. I hemmed and hawed and said, 'But...'

'Eat it!' he said, this time more emphatically.

As soon as I heard his emphatic tone, I involuntarily placed the bitter apple in my mouth. Ahmad swallowed his saliva and inched back a bit. When I placed the bitter apple in my mouth, I found it to be so sweet, crisp and juicy, so much so that I had never tasted a fruit as sweet and delicious as that bitter apple in my whole life. I wolfed down the other half before one could say *bismillāh ar-rahmān ar-rahīm (in the name of God, the Beneficent, the Merciful)*. When I swallowed the second half, Ahmad asked, 'How was it?'

I said, 'Amazing!' And then I turned to the man and said, 'Thank you, kind sir. It tasted great.'

The man did the same thing with the other bitter apple and gave it to Ahmad. When I saw how ravenously he ate his bitter apple, I thought that we

---

² Colocynth (Citrullus colocynthis).

The Fourteenth Tale

must look like a couple of impolite ruffians and felt ashamed.

The man asked, 'Has your thirst been quenched?'

Ahmad wiped his mouth with his sleeve and said, 'Absolutely!" Our thirst has been quenched, and our hunger has been satiated, too. Thank you very much indeed.'

The man placed a hand on his knee and stood up. His rising up was like the motion of a cloud, slow and rhythmic. He said, 'I'm going to leave now, but will return at the same time tomorrow.' With that, he mounted his sorrel, the like of which I had never seen before. The other man hurried forward and gave his lance for the young man to hold while he mounted his own white steed. I ran and caught a corner of the man's robe and said, 'Sir! For the love of God 🌼, take us to our homes.'

Ahmad ran and joined me and said, 'Just show us the way. Our parents will be very concerned for us.'

The man ran his hand over my head and said, 'You will go back at the appointed hour,' and drew a large circle around us with his lance. He then spurred his horse on and started on his way.

Ahmad ran after him and shouted, 'Sir! Please don't leave us alone here! Predators will tear us to pieces!'

My heart fluttered as I said, 'This would be a worse fate than dying of thirst.' I ran as I was saying this so that I could grab hold of the man's robe once again and plead with him. He stared at us in an assertive way that imbued him with such authority that we were powerless to do or say anything more. He then said, 'As long as you remain within the confines of that circle, you will be safe. Now go back.'

I said, 'Yes, sir.'

I was scared. I thought to myself, 'What kind of a person is this whom I love at first sight, but of whom I am also frightened?!'

The two riders disappeared behind the farthest dune. Ahmad was dumbstruck and didn't move a muscle.

I said, 'What a man! He was so awe-inspiring.'

Ahmad let out a deep sigh and sat in the middle of the circle. I couldn't peel my eyes from the path they had taken. Gone were the feelings of hunger and exhaustion. I didn't even have any fear of the predators that roamed the desert at night. A blissful serenity had come over my soul.'

I said, 'May God ❀ bless his heart. He brought us back to life.'

I bent over and ran my fingers over the delicate circle that he had made in the sand. My heart was filled with joy when I recalled his strong arms and magnetic eyes. I sat next to Ahmad, put my arm around his neck, and said, 'Aren't you happy?'

He said, 'Maybe that man wasn't a human being. Maybe he was an angel, or... I don't know, something else!'

The Fourteenth Tale

I said, 'That's possible. He had such a handsome face, such strong arms, and he had an incredibly pleasant aroma about him. Did you see his shoulders? If we placed both our shoulders together, they would still be thinner than his.' Then I laughed at the way we had wolfed down the bitter apples.

Ahmad laughed too. He was feeling much better. He said, 'Or maybe the Apostle of God ﷺ had sent him.'

I said, 'I feel so close to God ﷻ now.'

Without even a little bit of shame, I asked Ahmad, 'Do you know how to make your prayers properly and completely?'

Contrary to my expectations, he was not surprised. He smiled kindly and said, 'Well, we don't have any water, so we have to make our ablutions with this sand here.'

We performed our ritual ablutions and stood in the posture of prayer. Ahmad recited the prayers, and I repeated after him. We pronounced God's ﷻ proper name as it should be pronounced: Allāh, because we knew that God ﷻ could hear us and was listening. The sun was setting, and its heat was no longer oppressive. We talked non-stop about the young man who saved our lives until nightfall; about how young he was, how handsome, and how loving and kind. When we finished saying everything we could think of about him, we started from the top all over again! We had forgotten all about the fact that night had fallen and that we were stuck in the middle of a desert that was full of wolves

The Fourteenth Tale

and jackals that came out at night. We didn't even give a thought to what would happen tomorrow, what our parents would be thinking, or whether or not we would go hungry and thirsty again.

Although the moon was not full that night, we could nevertheless see each other and our surroundings with relative ease by starlight. I was seated facing Ahmad. He had cradled his knees with his arms, rocking gently back and forth, talking about what we should tell the man when we saw him again, what we should do, and what we should ask him. Then I noticed something lurking behind Ahmad, and I froze. Some wraith-like creatures were moving about not far from us. Their eyes shone in the darkness. I jumped up and yelled, 'Wolves!'

Ahmad got up too and stood next to me.

Scared, I asked, 'What should we do?'

Ahmad said, 'Keep calm.'

But I couldn't keep calm. Gone was my courage and self-assurance. I just wanted to flee from those white fangs that were approaching us at speed. I yelled, 'Run, Ahmad! They're going to be upon us at any moment!' But Ahmad grabbed my arm and forced me to sit down and said, 'Don't you move a muscle. Have you forgotten what the man said?'

I struggled to get free of him, yelling, 'Let go of me! Let me *go!* They're about to tear us to pieces!!'

Ahmad took me by the shoulders and shook me hard and said, 'Where do you want to run to, you fool? Take a look around you!'

The Fourteenth Tale

He was right. The wolves came closer and surrounded us. They were staring at us with their scary, shining eyes. We could even hear their panting and growling. I was shivering from fright and felt like I was being strangled by the lump that had formed in my throat. Instead, it made me burst into tears, which came rushing out as if a floodgate had been opened. I was clinging to Ahmad's arm and thinking that it would be good if they strangled me first so that I would die a quick death. Ahmad was shivering but kept quiet.

Eventually, the leader of the pack of wolves stepped forward. I squeezed my face against Ahmad's shoulder and yelled, 'No!... No!"

The Fourteenth Tale

I was expecting sharp fangs and claws to pierce my flesh at any moment, but that didn't happen. Ahmad let out the breath he had been holding in his chest from sheer fright, and stammered, "L-look!"

I couldn't believe what I was seeing with my own eyes. The wolves attacked, but just before their jaws reached the invisible line that the man had drawn in the sand, it was as if an invisible hand was holding them back!

Elated, Ahmad kept repeating, 'See? Now do you see I was right?'

He sat down and sat me down with him. It was a bizarre feeling. Even though I was seeing it with my own eyes, it was still an unbelievable sight. Miracles are like that. I was already feeling so much better. And seeing the frustrated look on the wolves' faces, who could smell the scent of our flesh and see it before their eyes, ready for the taking, yet they're not able to get at us—that made us feel even better. I said, 'Wow! What an incredible situation. To be within a couple of feet of a pack of ravenous wolves, and yet be safe...'

Ahmad said, 'So this is yet another miracle. Now I have no doubt that that man was from another world.'

A thought came into my mind, and I said, 'What if he is the spirit of one of the past prophets who has come down from Heaven to save us?'

'The more we think about it, the more confused we'll become. Let's just wait and ask him who he is tomorrow.'

He pointed at the wolves and said, 'Look. They've given up!'

The wolves had given up their attempts to get at us and were rubbing their jaws on the ground and sulking away. I lay down on my back, and Ahmad did the same. The desert sky was filled with a canopy of stars, alive with shooting stars whizzing by, almost with every breath we took.

I said, 'When I think about how close God 🌼 is to us and that He is watching over our every move, it gives me a sense of peace and serenity.'

Ahmad replied, 'If everyone had that same feeling, no one would ever commit a sin.'

A comet flew across the sky and made its way down to the horizon. Then, a sadness swept over me.

I said, 'I know, Ahmad. Up until now, I couldn't even perform my prayers properly. I was never conscious of God 🌼 the way I should have been, but He helped me. He helped us both by sending that man to save us.'

Ahmad said, 'I'm the same way, Mahmoud. If it weren't for my father forcing me to do the right thing, I wouldn't be someone who performed his prayers regularly and properly either.' He then sat up and asked, 'Will you pray with me now?'

No suggestion would have made me happier at that moment on that magical night. Praying under that canopy of stars and comets, and being so conscious of God 🌼, who we felt so close to, had a completely different, other-worldly feel to it. After we offered our

The Fourteenth Tale

prayers to our Creator, we fell into a deep and peaceful sleep, not giving any thought to the wolves or the cold of the desert at night, neither of which affected us within the protective dome that had been made for us.

When I was asleep, I felt like someone was tickling my foot. I said, 'Don't, Mom! I'm still sleepy.'

I turned to my side and saw my mother carrying a large pot of water and placing it on the stove next to where I was sleeping. My mother put the pot on my chest. I tried to get out from under its burden but was powerless to do so. I pleaded with her, but she just increased the pressure on the pot. I couldn't breathe or let out a sound.

I suddenly woke up and saw Ahmad's face, who had fallen over me. Before I had had a chance to register a protest, Ahmad said, 'Shhh! Be still and don't move! There's a scorpion on your leg.'

I was still groggy with sleep, but hearing the word "scorpion" brought me to my senses immediately, and I raised my upper body a little without moving my legs to get a better look. One of my legs had drifted outside our protective circle while I was asleep, and a large golden scorpion was crawling along it.

Ahmad said, 'Don't move!'

He got up, rolled his keffiyeh into a rattail, and whipped the scorpion with it. But the scorpion didn't fall outside the circle but clung to the keffiyeh and then fell to the ground inside the circle. We moved away from it. The scorpion was making strange movements, as if in agony. It eventually left the circle and disappeared.

Ahmad said, 'Remember, we can't put a foot outside our protective circle until the Master returns.'

'Master?' I asked, surprised.

Ahmad smiled and said, 'Isn't that an appropriate title for someone who has saved us from certain death and all these dangers?'

I nodded my agreement. I liked that title and repeated the word several times. It was truly a title worthy of the man. By now, the sun had dawned and risen up, and although I knew that the weather was as hot as it was yesterday, I didn't feel hot or thirsty. We didn't even feel hungry. But the more time passed and the longer the day became, the thirstier we became to see our Master's face and eyes. A strange anxiety came over me once the sun had passed its midpoint and was waning towards its setting on the horizon. I couldn't sit still or stand and stare at the horizon, which is what Ahmad was doing. What if our Master didn't show up? What if he forgot about us? Do we need to make more supplications to ensure that he comes back? These were the thoughts that were passing through my mind.

I couldn't stand it any longer and said, 'What if he doesn't show up??'

Ahmad understood my concern and said, 'As long as we stay within this circle, we'll be safe. Someone is bound to pass by here eventually.' He then added dejectedly, 'But it would be a great shame if he didn't show up and we don't see him again.'

'That's my whole point,' I protested. 'I am prepared to die, as long as I can see our Master's beatific countenance and sense his presence one more time.'

After I said that, I suddenly saw the dust cloud that the horses' hooves of the two riders were raising as they approached us. They were sauntering at such a gentle pace that I thought they'd never get to us. I felt like my heart was going to burst out of my ribcage; it was beating so excitedly. My arms and legs were quivering, and I knew that Ahmad wasn't feeling any different.

They finally arrived and dismounted a few feet away from us. Ahmad ran forward and offered his *salām*, after which I regained my composure and did the same. The young man's face was covered by the tail end of his green turban, which he uncovered by pulling it aside, revealing his handsome face. He smiled and returned our *salāms*. I took a step forward and saw that Ahmad had gone to bend down so that he could kiss his hand, but the Master raised him up and caressed his hair instead. I involuntarily took in a deep breath to take in his scent and said, 'I missed you so much.'

He said, 'I know... you missed the feeling of being close to God ☙, which is why you were so earnest in the prayers you offered last night. Allow me to offer my prayers too, and later...'

Our master's squire had laid down a prayer mat of green velvet, the like of which I had never seen before, and the strange thing was that it was large enough to accommodate more than two people.

The Fourteenth Tale

The man in white recited the *adhān*, the call to prayer. He repeated the formula *ḥayya 'alā khayr al-'amal* (Hurry toward the best of deeds) with such an emphatic tone that we thought that he was inviting us to join them in their prayers.

I said to Ahmad, 'Does he mean that we should join them too?'

Ahmad replied, 'Whatever he means, I for one will be joining them!'

I pointed at the way they held their hands, and said, 'Look! They are Shī'a.'

Their hands were held straight down at their sides in the Shī'a style, rather than folded over their bellies.[3]

Ahmad hesitated for a few moments, then shrugged his shoulders as if to say it didn't matter to him, and then took his position behind our Master. I did the same, thinking about each and every word of the prayer. I was able to recite the entirety of the prayers without any pauses or errors for the first time ever. It was the most beautiful and sincere prayers that I had

---

[3] Most Sunnis, with the notable exception of the Mālikis, fold their hands over their bellies when they stand in prayer. The Mālikis are an exception to this, following the example of their imām, Mālik ibn Anas, who lived in Medina and who therefore knew how all Medinans prayed, following the example of the Prophet, of course. Mālik ibn Anas predated the founders of the other three Sunni rites (none of whom lived in Medina, in which case they would have learned how the people of 'The City of the Prophet' (Medina) prayed, and today, everyone would be praying the way the Prophet and the Imams prayed in Medina, i.e. like the Shī'a and the Mālikis.

ever made in my whole life. I still envy the abilities that I had on that occasion.

After we had made our prayers, we sat kneeling before our Master, who said with the most heart-warming smile, 'Well, my dear friends, tell me how you spent the night.'

Ahmad said, 'Very comfortably. We didn't even feel any hunger or thirst, or the cold of the desert at night. However, your absence was sorely felt. I'm sure that you know full well all about our condition.'

And I added, 'These miracles of yours are feats that are the exclusive domain of the prophets...'

The young man smiled and, after a long pause, said, 'But as you know, [the office of] prophethood came to a close after the prophethood of the Prophet Muḥammad ﷺ. The man whom you have chosen to refer to as 'Master' is not a prophet, but rather, is a progeny of a prophet.'

I nudged Ahmad and said, 'See? What did I say? He knows that we call him "Master".'

Ahmad asked, 'To which of the prophets does your lineage go back to?'

He smiled and said, 'To my lord and master Muḥammad al-Muṣṭafā (Muḥammad, the Chosen One), unto whom be God's ﷻ peace, for all eternity.'

I asked, 'Who is your father?'

'Ḥasan, the son of Ali.'

Ahmad said in surprise, 'The Imam of the Shī'a?' And then he just gaped at the Imam. He then said, 'The Imam of the Shī'a that they say... is somehow hidden from public view?'

The Imam said, 'Is that what you think? Am I hidden from your view, or can you see me?'

Tears started to flow from Ahmad's eyes, and he said, 'My father rejects the Shī'a belief in your reality.' He then slapped his knee hard and said, 'Oh, father! I wish you were here now so that you could see with your own eyes the person in whose reality you do not believe.'

Our Master placed a hand on Ahmad's shoulder and said gently, 'If you come to believe in what you see with your own eyes, your father will also come to believe in me.'

Ahmad said through a veil of tears, 'Master! How is it even possible for me to doubt what I see with my own eyes? I might have doubts about who *I* am, but I can never doubt who *you* are!'

Tears had gathered in my eyes too, and now they flowed down my cheeks. I said, 'And even if Ahmad has any doubts, I have no doubts about who you are.' I said this, bent over, and kissed his blessed hand. He caressed my head then, and the feeling I got when he did that was a feeling of love for which I had been searching in vain in my parents.

He then said, 'Do you not want to eat another bitter apple?'

'Anything that comes from you is good and pure,' Ahmad replied.

Our master took a couple of bitter apples from his squire, rotated them in his hands, split them in two, then gave them to us and said, 'I will be leaving now. But don't worry. You will be rescued from here in about an hour.'

We ate the bitter apples, and although they were sweet and juicy, they didn't taste as good as they had yesterday because the thought of our Master leaving was more bitter than the sweetness of their taste.

Through my tears, I managed to ask, 'Will we ever see you again?'

Ahmad fell to the Master's feet and pleaded, 'Won't you take us with you?'

The Master caressed Ahmad's head and said, 'Whensoever you call to me from the bottom of your heart, you will see me. You will be [a part] of me; Ahmad sooner, and Mahmoud later.'

He rose up slowly, as did his squire. I pleaded, 'Master!'

I wanted to grab the velvet prayer mat, but there was no longer any such thing, and before I knew it, they were already mounted on their horses. Ahmad was just standing there, dumbfounded. Our Master raised his hand in a gesture of farewell and took off. I ran after them, yelling, 'Don't forget us!'

My eyes followed them until they eventually disappeared over the last dune in the far distance.

The Fourteenth Tale

3

We were "corpses who came back from the dead". This is what the old man who found us said, who spent his days in the desert gathering thornbushes, driftwood, and other kindling to sell for a living. He stopped his work to take us back and deliver us to our families so that he might get a reward and, as he put it, have a feast for a day instead of just making ends meet. It was hard for me to step out of that circle. When Ahmad restored a portion of the circle that had been covered with sand by the wind, I wondered if it would retain its protective qualities for others. As a farewell ritual, I bent down and kissed a part of the circle, then followed the old man as he led us back home. Now that we had been found, instead of revelling at the prospect of being reunited with our families, we pined for the person whom we had lost, who had disappeared behind the sand dune that we had left behind.

The Fourteenth Tale

The Fourteenth Tale

4

My mother poured some pomegranate juice for my father, who had taken to shaking his head and tut-tutting after hearing my story. Mother said, 'The kid's suffered from so much sunstroke that it has fried his brains!'

Father took another sip of the pomegranate juice and said, 'It's not unlikely. Remember Salīm and how delirious he had become after he spent all day in the sun? There was no end to the nonsense he spewed!' He then offered me some of his pomegranate juice, saying, 'Drink up, my boy. You're suffering a bad case of sunstroke and are delirious.'

The doctor put down his large leatherbound book and lowered the corners of his mouth at the same time as raising his eyebrows. He snapped my lower eyelid back into place after finally letting it go, and said, 'These kinds of words are attributes of his age and the phase he is passing through. All boys suffer from delusions and fantastic thoughts before they fully mature. They find things that set them apart from the crowd or make them feel special. Or they sometimes act like simpletons and morons to garner the sympathy of their friends and family... What did you say you ate in the desert?'

'Bitter apples,' I replied. I wanted to say how sweet they tasted, and that this was one of the miracles of the Master, but the doctor didn't give me a chance, and said, 'Ah, there you have it then, that makes it even worse. Have you not heard that bitter apples contain a potent toxin that debilitates the mind?'

My mother hit herself on the head and yelled out, 'Oh, how my poor little child has suffered from so much hunger and thirst that he has had to eat that bitter poison or whatever it's called!'

I said, 'To the contrary, we neither suffered from hunger nor any thirst thanks to the bitter apples that the Master gave us to eat. And they were even very...'

My father interrupted me, saying, 'I don't want to hear that nonsense coming out of you again, do you hear?!' He then turned to the doctor and said, 'Have mercy on us! My boy is losing his mind!'

The doctor took out a small sack from his pocket and gave it to my father and said, 'This medicine is foul-smelling and tastes bad too, but it will have a fantastic invigorating effect on your boy! It will act as an antidote to the bitter apple toxicity and will cure him of his delirium, too.'

I wanted to protest that I was not raving, and that everything that I said we had seen was true. Still, I feared that another sack of medicine would be added to cure my talking too much, in addition to the one I had already been prescribed.

When the doctor left, I expected my father to continue his aggressive behaviour towards me, but he just turned to me and said, 'I would have preferred it for you to have remained dead than for people to say you have gone mad. Stop your madness and put an end to this nonsense that you are saying. Do I make myself *perfectly* clear?'

I wanted to protest, but my father raised his hand and yelled, 'Not another word! Even if everything you say is true, I don't want you to say a single word about it to anyone. I don't want them to think you have become Shī'a. As God ﷻ is my witness, if I hear another word out of you about your so-called "Master", I will personally draw and tie your limbs to four posts in the middle of that desert and let the sun roast you like a rack of lamb! And if I see you associating with this Ahmad fellow one more time, I'll break both your legs! Is that clear?!'

He was so angry, and his voice was so frightening that I automatically nodded my ascent and glanced at my mother so that she might intervene, but the anger in her eyes was on a par with that of my father's.

Was it even possible for me not to look Ahmad up and see how he was doing? Of course not! Especially as the word on the grapevine was that Ahmad and Mahmoud had gone crazy, and that Ahmad was done for. These rumours were repeated so much that even I began to have doubts that maybe I had become delirious and that it was the effect of the sunstroke I had suffered.

The key to unravelling the mystery was with Ahmad, and I used the opportunity of a day when my father was absent to pay Ahmad a visit. Contrary to my expectations, he was neither depressed nor disturbed. I had never seen him so alive and full of verve. He embraced me passionately, kissed both my cheeks, and said, 'It's been hard on you, hasn't it?'

I said, 'What they did to me, they wouldn't have done to the wolves of the desert. I don't dare to leave the house! When I do, I hear people saying 'Crazy... crazy' so many times that I have no choice but to go back inside. What's more, my father has made me promise not to say a word about what happened to anyone and has especially sworn me off seeing you. To tell you the truth, doubt has crept into my own mind, too, Ahmad. Could it be that we imagined everything, and that none of it was real? Could it all have been the result of the sunstroke?'

Ahmad took hold of my arm and said, 'We can't talk here. Let's head out to the palm plantation.'

So, we headed out there. The dates were hanging in bunches that ranged in a spectrum of colour from tan to amber and brown. We found a couple of trees whose trunks were in the shade and sat, leaning against them, facing each other. Ahmad was silent. I don't know what he was thinking of, but he had a smile on his face.

I asked, 'Did they have the doctor come and see you, too?'

He nodded, smiled, and said, 'Wow! What a doctor. He wanted to force some concoction down my throat. He said that if I had been with you and had eaten bitter apples too, he had to give me the antidote before I went completely bonkers.' He chuckled and said, 'But my father set him straight. He said, "I don't know what my son has or hasn't seen, but one thing I am sure of is that I have never seen him feel so good in his whole life".'

I said, 'What do you mean? Didn't you tell him everything that happened?'

He said, 'Of course! How could I *not* tell him? Needless to say, my father did advise me not to repeat the story to anyone else. He says it is dangerous and will do nothing but cause me trouble. But he was taken by it *himself!* He went right to his books and spent the whole day leafing through them. Sometime after the sun had set and he had burned through a candle or two, he finally said he had found the identity of our Master.'

I felt hot in my head. I swallowed hard and said, 'Here I am thinking that I should come and see you to confirm my suspicions that what we had seen was nothing but a delusion, and now you tell me that your father has found out who the Master is??'

A small stalk of dates fell to the ground, not far from where we were sitting. Ahmad stood to pick it up and said, 'So it seems they have given you a tough time, because what happened to us was not something that one can easily harbour doubts about or forget about its significance. Don't you remember the Master's beautiful countenance and the amazing scent that surrounded him like an aura? Can you really forget that wonderful scent so soon?'

I picked a date from the stalk that Ahmad had extended towards me and placed it in my mouth. It was very sweet, and its sweetness reminded me of the sweetness of the bitter apples that had quenched our thirst and sated our hunger in that desert. And then my nostrils were filled with the pleasant scent of our Master, and that took me back to our experience, which brought tears to my eyes. I said, 'How can I forget that? Tell me what your father said about him.'

Ahmad gave me a stalk of dates. His face was ablaze, and his eyes glimmered. My father said the same thing that the Master himself had said, that his attributes were a match to the Imam of the Shī'a who is absent or in a state of 'occultation' as they say, and that he is the son of their Eleventh Imam, Imām Ḥasan al-'Askarī ﷺ. He is known by several names and titles. His name is Muḥammad ﷺ, and he is known as the Mahdī or the Ḥujjah. Do you remember when he said he was

The Fourteenth Tale

the son of Ḥasan ibn Ali ﷺ? Remember the miracles he performed for us? My father said that he is not bound by the limitations of time and space as we are.'

I said, 'But we aren't Shī'a, so why did he come to our aid?'

Ahmad jumped up, clapped his hands together in excitement, and said, 'My father said that he is God's ﷻ *walī*[4] on earth who comes to the aid of anyone who is in need, regardless of his religion. I can't tell you how excited I am. I miss him so much! I want to head out and get lost in the desert again so that I can call out to him and cry and supplicate and plead so much that he will come to my aid again, after which I will never let him out of my sight for a single moment, even if I have to follow him to the end of the world. I want to be like his squire, the man in white. Did you see how he looked

---

[4] *Walī* 1. regent, sovereign, lord and master; 2. patron, guardian, protector, custodian. The plural form of *walī* is *awliyā'*: those of God's ﷻ creatures who have spiritual proximity to Him, inclusive of prophets and Imāms and, to a lesser degree, the *ulamā* and *fuqahā*; in a distant sense: "saints". The *walī* is usually an abbreviation of *walī al-amr*, who is the Just Ruler and Guardian-Sovereign of the affairs of the believers. *Walī*: In most Shi'a contexts, *walī* or *walī al-amr* refers to the Just Ruler who is divinely appointed to interpret and implement His will over the community of those who have self-surrendered their will unto Him, i.e. appointed to rule over the community of the faithful.

Walīyic: endowed with or having to do with *wilāyah* (Persian: *velāyat*); the legitimate guardianship-type authority to act as leader of the community of the faithful on behalf of the Imam of the Age ﷺ in his physical absence while the Era of the Occultation lasts; guardianship-type regency.

at the master? I'm going to head out there one day soon, you'll see. My father has attained to faith in the Master, too! He says that he knows that I will no longer be able to resist going after him, and that one day I will leave to go and find him.'

Ahmad's passion scared me more than it engendered empathy. I said, 'Do you really intend to leave? What about your family? What if you do get lost and the Master doesn't come to help you this time? What will you do then?'

I thought of my father and the anger in his eyes. Ahmad was staring at me with a strange sort of smile on his face. There was nothing but pity in his eyes. He came up to me, placed a hand on my shoulder, and said, 'Here's another example of how what the Master said has come to pass. He said, "Ahmad sooner, and Mahmoud later". No, my dear Mahmoud. I have no doubt about the matter. If I call out to him from the very core of my being, he will respond.' And then he suddenly embraced me and squeezed me against his chest, and said, 'I'll miss you. You are the only person in this world with whom I share this secret, which is why you are the dearest person in the world to me. May God ❦ keep you and bless you.'

I felt like going with him so that we could supplicate to the Imam together. But the vision of the anger in my father's eyes when he ordered me not to repeat my experience appeared before my eyes and prevented me from even thinking about going with Ahmad. It pained me to think about the possibility of

The Fourteenth Tale

Ahmad leaving and not being able to see him again. I don't know why I felt that if Ahmad left, my certainty about seeing our Master would turn into nothing more than a figment of my imagination, which is just what my parents accused me of harbouring.

The Fourteenth Tale

The Fourteenth Tale

5

Mahmoud became silent then and stared out the window. Years had passed since the events he recounted, and he now had a son who entered the room carrying a tray with a large platter of watermelon slices. The fragrance of the watermelon made my mouth water; it was very sweet and really hit the spot. As I took in another mouthful of the delicious fruit, I asked, 'Were the bitter apples that you ate as cold and refreshing and sweet as this watermelon?' Mahmoud the Persian said, 'They were actually sweeter and better tasting than any fruit that can be found on Earth.'

I said, 'You told me you are a *shī'a* (follower or partisan) of Imam Ali . How was it that you later decided to join the ranks of the Shī'a?'

Muslim took a bite out of a slice of watermelon, and then said, 'The rest of the story has yet to be told; it's too bad I have to leave, but you have to promise you'll tell me the rest of the story later.'

Mahmoud said, 'God ﷻ knows how many times you've heard me tell this story, but you are still passionate about it and shed tears every time, just like you did when you heard me tell it the first time.'

Muslim placed a hand on his knee, rose up and said, 'I'll want to hear it again, even after I've heard it a thousand times. So, take care of our scribe here, and think about the blessing that will accrue from the number of people who will be affected by reading your story.'

I got up and bade Muslim farewell. Mahmoud went with him up to the door of the house's courtyard. When he returned to the living room, I was taken aback by the awe that the luminosity of his countenance inspired in me. I thought, 'If this is the kind of person the Imam's followers are like, then what would the Imam himself be like?!' When Mahmoud returned, his son got up to leave, but Mahmoud called him back, saying, 'Mahdi, come back here.'

Mahdi came back and gave his father a nice smile. He came closer, and then, at his father's prompting, placed his head on his father's thigh. Mahmoud then turned to me and said, 'You must be tired... Would you like to hear the rest of the story some other day?'

The Fourteenth Tale

'Not at all! If you knew how eager I am to hear the rest of the story, you wouldn't have paused even for a moment; unless you are tired yourself, of course.'

He shook his head, and while he was caressing Mahdi's head, he said, 'No... I'm just saddened when I think of all the years I spent in bewilderment, while knowing what the right path was; although nothing comes of ruing what could have been.'

The Fourteenth Tale

The Fourteenth Tale

6

I had bought some pack mules and camels with the capital that my father had left me and which I had been able to save. I'd hire these animals out to travellers and pilgrims who wanted to go on pilgrimage from Ḥillah to Kāẓimayn and Sāmarrā. I would have to go with them, of course, to tend to the animals and act as their guide. Some of these travellers, especially the merchants and the well-to-do, thought that they had hired me along with the pack animals. They would order me about, stint on the rental amount, and generally make a nuisance of themselves, causing great frustration for me.

I remember one occasion; it was when I had just returned from Kāẓimayn. My travelling companions were merchants who brought merchandise from

The Fourteenth Tale

Kāẓimayn to Ḥillah. In addition to treating me as nothing more than a servant who was at their beck and call, they had also overloaded my pack mules and camels to the point of their exhaustion. They ultimately underpaid me, which caused a bitter quarrel between us. But no matter how much I pleaded and then yelled, it didn't make a damned bit of difference. The head of their caravan said, "It is what it is", and that he would not pay a single dinar more.

For my part, when I saw that it was useless to keep arguing my case with them, I just went and sat on one of those low, wood-planked platforms and brooded. I was so livid that I was probably frothing at the mouth with anger, and my soul was in even worse shape; it was on fire. My camels and mules were lying down on the ground from exhaustion. I took off my turban, unravelled it, and used it to dry the sweat off my face and neck. Then my eyes fell on the clothes of a man dressed in white whose clothing fluttered in the wind. I raised my head and saw that the clothes belonged to a man who was lean and tall, with a brown beard and hair, whose smile calmed me a little.

He said, 'Are you Mahmoud the Persian? I hear you hire out pack animals; is that right?'

'Yes, I'm Mahmoud the Persian,' I replied, 'but no, I don't have any pack animals for hire. I'm sorry. The last caravan of travellers was so horrible that I've decided to pack up the business and not have to deal with its hassles anymore. Go and get your animals from someone else, if you please.'

The Fourteenth Tale

The man replied mildly and with kindness in his tone of voice, 'Yes, but the others are not Mahmoud the Persian, who has a reputation of being able to get us to Sāmarrā in the shortest possible time.'

It was as if he had rubbed salt in my wound. I said, 'Sure, that's the service I give, but you saw the thanks I got.'

A big smile came on his face, revealing a set of teeth that were as white as pearls. He said, 'People are different. Our party consists of a few Shī'a pilgrims who want to get to Sāmarrā, and we will pay you your fee in advance, at whatever rate you set yourself. Now be a good fellow and don't turn us down.'

His voice was so pleasing to my ears that it sweetened the sour taste that my experience with the last set of travellers had left in my mouth. I said, 'Well, right now, my animals are too tired to be able to do anything anyway. I will be taking them to the watering hole in the morning. Be there then if you want to know about my decision.'

'Bless your heart,' he said, and took his leave, with the wind raising the hem of his gown and making it flutter about him.

The hardest part of this job is taking the animals to the spring and grooming them. You have to coax them into going into the water, and once you have prevailed upon them to do so, you can't get them to come out. This was especially true of a stubborn male camel I had, who would start kicking and biting as soon as he saw a body of water. No matter what trick I tried,

I could not get him to bathe. It was this same story all over again the last time, and as a result, his whole body was covered with ticks and mites. I tried to goad him on by hitting him with a cane, but he would growl at me and raise his lips up as if getting ready to bite me, baring his teeth. If I were nice to him and caressed him, he would buck and kick out his rear legs. He frustrated me so much that he eventually drove me to yell at him and curse him. Then I heard a voice say, 'Why do you curse one of God's creatures?'

It was the same man who had approached me yesterday. This time, he was accompanied by a slightly shorter companion who wore a green turban. I said, 'This animal brings out the worst in me. No matter what I do, I can't get him to go into the water. I'm concerned that his ticks and mites will infect the other animals too.'

'You are right to be concerned,' the man said as he rolled up his sleeves. You are tired, and these poor beasts of burden are exhausted, too. And it's challenging to do your job on your own. Here, I'll give you a hand.'

'No, that's ok,' I said. 'There's no need for you to put yourself through the bother, brother... I don't even know your name.'

He said, 'I'm Ja'far, the son of Khālid. And this brother of mine is Muḥammad, the son of Yāsir. Nor is it any bother. If we don't help our brothers in faith, then what good does it do to be a Muslim in the first place?'

He stepped forward and grabbed my camel's reins at the camel's mouth in one quick motion. The camel pulled away, being his usual stubborn self. But Ja'far started to talk to the animal in a way you'd talk to a human being. He continued talking to him in the same gentle manner and gradually coaxed him into the water. And for his part, Muḥammad waded into the water, too, and started grooming the animals, as if he were grooming his own. The male camel continued to be refractory, pulling his head back, but his recalcitrance had lost its vehemence. In any event, he had made Ja'far go waist-deep into the water. Once he had been able to coax the camel into the water, the animal began to enjoy the feel of it and immersed his head and neck deep into it. I laughed and said, 'It seems, Ja'far *Āqā* (sir), that it is your lot for this animal to bear you to Sāmarrā in gratitude for what you have done for him!'

Muḥammad said, 'May the Lord be praised that you consented to take us; *al-ḥamdulillāh.*'

I said, 'Up until yesterday, I was at the service of lords. But as of today, I will be at the service of my brothers [in faith].'

We agreed to set off in two days. No matter how much I insisted on getting no more than half of the fee up front and the other half when we got there, they would not agree to that and paid the whole amount up front. That was very reassuring and made me very happy. I couldn't really figure out *why* it made me so happy, because it wasn't really on account of their paying me upfront; knowing the kind of people they were, I had no doubt that I would eventually be paid my due in full and would not be shortchanged. They seemed to me to be true believers, and it had been years since such people had come across the trajectory of my life. My own faith and the practice of my religion had come down to performing the five daily ritual devotions, and fasting during the blessed month of Ramaḍān, and these I did only because of my fear of the Day of Judgment and the fires of Hell.

There were fourteen of them, which made us fifteen, with me acting as their guide. Whenever I glanced back at the face of any one of them, he would give me such a sincere and kindly smile that it made me feel ashamed [of the crudity of my own character]. Ja'far was riding that same stubborn camel, who had calmed down considerably and was sauntering along just fine. Around noon, we reached a small oasis and stopped to make our noon prayers and to have something to eat. Before I had had a chance, the travellers themselves had sat the pack animals down, whereas this was one of my duties, not theirs. They made their ritual devotions communally, and I made mine on my own. As it was my habit, I sat down in some corner and opened my bundle of bread and dates. After I had placed the first morsel of bread and dates in my mouth, I noticed that all my travel companions, who were sitting around their table spread, were staring at me without having touched their own food.

'Please begin your meal,' I said.

The Fourteenth Tale

Their elder, whose name was Sayyāh, said, 'What are you doing sitting there, eating on your own? As God ﷻ is my witness, we will not start eating until you come and join us.'

Muḥammad came over and said in a friendly tone, 'Hmm. Let me see what it is that you are eating. Something better than what we have, no doubt!'

I felt ashamed. I gathered my bundle of bread and dates and went over and joined them. Their food was the same as mine, but their dates were *rutab* varieties, whereas mine were *khārak*.[5] I can't remember how long it had been since a meal had tasted so good to me. The words that were exchanged and their sense of humour was heart-warming. They treated me no differently than any other member of their own party. After the meal, they made *chāy*, a stimulating brew of steeped herbs that really invigorated me. We set off again on a journey I didn't want to end, so I wouldn't be deprived of seeing those luminous faces and being in the company of these wonderful pilgrims.

After the passage of a few days in their company, I had grown used to them, and a strong liking for them had found its way into my heart. I especially liked the way they performed their ritual devotions and supplications, as well as their supererogatory night-

---

[5] The difference is in the level of the maturation of the date fruit. *Khārak* is an unripe date that is dry and astringent, whereas *rutab* dates are more mature, sweeter, moister, and softer. *Khārak* dates are much lighter in color, being light tan, whereas *rutab* dates are a deep brown color.

time supplications and psalm recitals. I was so taken by their rituals and devotions that it was hard for me not to participate in performing them with them, as I did when I shared their meals and sleeping quarters with them.

I could not sleep at all the last night I was with them. I was feeling down, gazing at the night sky, which was brimming with stars. That was nothing new; there were many nights that I spent alone, gazing at the stars. But on that night, the people who were sleeping next to me had filled the vacuity of my sense of loneliness. Never in my whole life had I felt so much love for, and a sense of being drawn to people, as I felt about this company of men on that night.

I felt sure that it was the strength of the faith of these fourteen Shī'a men that had made such an impression on me. There was such a great distance between us in terms of the strength of our faith. In my travels, I had seen many people of different sects and denominations. Yet even those who were Sunni and were also of the same religio-legal rite (*madhhab*) as I was never treated me the way these pilgrims had. A comet suddenly flew across the sky. The sky was a canopy of stars, and its beauty, together with the comet's passing and the feelings I had inside, reminded me of a distant memory — a memory in the corner of my mind. But no matter how hard I tried to recall it, I could not coax it to the forefront of my mind. I tried so hard to recall that memory that I eventually fell asleep.

The Fourteenth Tale

I dreamed I was in Heaven, next to some large trees with leaves of different colours, which bore various fruit. What was strange was that the trees and their roots were suspended in mid-air, and their branches were within easy reach, such that I could easily reach out and pick any fruit I wanted. Four rivulets passed around me, each of which flowed streams of water, milk, honey, and a sweet cordial or fruit squash. All you needed to do was kneel and drink your fill from whichever stream you desired. Some beautiful men and women ate of the fruit of the trees and drank from the streams. I reached out to pick one of the fruits, but suddenly the fruits moved away from me and were no longer in my reach. I then knelt to drink from one of the streams, and the same thing happened: the rivulets deepened, and their contents were no longer accessible to me.

I asked the people who were gathered there, 'Why is it that all of you can eat and drink here, but I cannot?'

They replied, 'Because you have yet to join us. You have not come here yet.'

Then I suddenly saw a group of people dressed in white who were coming towards us, and I heard voices in the crowd saying, 'It is our Lady, the daughter of the Prophet ﷺ, Lady Fāṭimah ﷺ, approaching.

There were many angels around Lady Fāṭimah ﷺ, and their numbers increased by the minute. When she was close to where I was standing, I saw a tall, broad-shouldered young man whose face seemed familiar to me. When he saw me, he gave me a big smile that warmed my heart. When I saw the look in his eyes, I suddenly remembered the experience Ahmad and I had had in that desert, and how we had almost died of thirst but had been saved by the Master.

A shiver ran through me in my dream. I heard the people say, 'He's Muḥammad, the son of Ḥasan ﷺ, the Awaited One who will Rise Up (*al-qā'im al-muntaẓar*).'

The people arose and greeted Lady Fāṭimah ﷺ, and I stood up too and said, 'Peace be unto you, O Daughter of the Prophet.'

She replied, 'And unto you be God's ﷻ peace, O Mahmoud. Are you not the same person whom this son of mine saved from that torment?'

I said, 'Indeed. He is my Master and saviour.'

She said, 'Do you not want to be covered under [the protection of] his aegis (*wilāyah*[6])?'

'That is my greatest desire,' I replied.

Lady Fāṭimah ﷺ smiled and said, 'Glad tidings to you, O Mahmoud, for you have [thereby] attained salvation.'

The look of my Master reminded me of a lifetime that was spent neglecting him. I ran forward in contrition, wanting to take his hand and ask for his forgiveness when I awoke.

---

[6] *Wilāyah*: Divinely sanctioned legal and moral authority or dominion.

The Fourteenth Tale

Ja'far was rubbing my shoulders gently and calling me. When I woke up, I said, 'I dreamed of your Imam and the daughter of the Prophet.'

Ja'far said, 'Take a deep breath, and then tell me all about it.'

He went and got me a cup of water. When I felt a little more relaxed, I told the story from its very beginning, from the time Ahmad and I got lost in that wilderness, and the miracle of the Master who saved us, all the way up to the dream that I had just had. Sayyāh embraced me in his arms and said, 'Truly, you have the scent of paradise about you. You must come with us tomorrow to the shrine of Imam Mūsā, the son of Ja'far ﷺ, and see our sheikh. I felt a special bond of friendship with you from the moment I saw you, and now I know the reason for it.'

Tears started rolling down my cheeks. I took hold of his hands and placed them on my eyes. I wanted to kiss his feet, but he didn't let me. He held me in his arms and we both wept profusely.

We went to the shrine of Imam Mūsā, the son of Ja'far ﷺ, on the morning of the following day. I kept repeating the invocation (*dhikr*) 'praise be unto God ﷻ' (*al-ḥamdulillāh*) for having guided me [aright]. The custodians of the shrine came to greet us. They told us that the sheikh has been anxiously awaiting a man by the name of Mahmoud all morning, whom, he says, is coming to join the friends of the Lord of the Age ﷺ. The custodians then told us that the sheikh had ordered them to treat Mahmoud with great respect and to take him to the sheikh. This was an example of an 'impossible wonder' (*karāmah*)[7] of the sheikh's, which brought tears of joy to the eyes of some of my companions. As for me, I was utterly beside myself in awe and amazement.

Ja'far held me by my arm and said, 'Come on, brother. Happy is your fate, for God ﷻ and the Imams ﷺ obviously have your back. Remember me when you get up there [to Heaven]!'

I sat down. I couldn't move. I was told that the sheikh was coming. When he got to me, he embraced me with such passion that it was as if he was giving a bear hug to someone he had known for years. There was something about him that seemed so familiar to me that it made it impossible to peel my eyes from him. Those eyes, and those eyebrows that touched each other in the middle, those narrow lips that were always smiling... They reminded me of someone... but who?? His face looked so familiar.

I said, 'Greetings, O sheikh. I have had a dream and an adventure which –'

He interrupted me and said, 'I know; I know. I know all about it. I know about your dream, your name and lineage, and I know all about your adventure too.

---

[7] *Karāma*: impossible wonders. God's ﷻ munificence in His granting supernatural knowledge or powers to those who have proximity to Him, other than prophets and Imams. These are so-called to distinguish them from miracles, which, strictly speaking, belong exclusively to prophets and Imams.

The Fourteenth Tale

Last night, the Lady of the Two Worlds[8] ﷻ came to me in a dream too, and said that my friend from our torment in the desert will be coming to see me, to join the ranks of her devotees, just as her son had stated. *Now* do you recognise me??'

I wanted to shout out with sheer joy. I cradled his face with both my hands and stared into his eyes. I said, 'Oh, my dear, dear Ahmad. My dear friend! Is it really *you* – the sheikh I've heard so much about?'

He said, 'I became a Shī'a many years ago, and I must tell you that I did indeed see our Master again and complained to him, asking him when he would finally have my friend join me. And praise be to God ﷻ, my prayers have been answered, and here you are!'

What could I say? I kissed his forehead and embraced him some more and praised God ﷻ for considering me worthy enough to be guided to the right path.

---

[8] The reference here is to Lady Fātima ﷻ, of course. The 'two worlds' refer to the physical world (*al-'ālam ash-shuhūd*), and the supra-sensible domain or the "metaphysical hypostasis" (as Henry Corbin refers to it); the underlying substantive domain that is beyond the ken of ordinary human perception (*al-'ālam al-ghayb*).

The Fourteenth Tale

7

Mahmoud the Persian had gone silent for a while and was staring at me. I had been carried away by the thoughts this story inspired. I snapped out of my thoughts and suddenly remembered the Fourteenth Tale, and said, 'Isn't it strange that my Fourteenth Tale should be about the Fourteenth Infallible, the Lord of the Age ?'

Mahmoud the Persian took both my hands in his and stared into my eyes. In the twilight of dusk, his eyes had an alluring glimmer to them. He said in a penetrating voice that had a slight quiver to it, 'No, it is not strange, my friend. If you attain faith in the reality of that great nobleman, you will know that there is no miracle that he cannot perform.'

I bowed down and kissed his hands. In return, he drew my head toward himself and kissed my forehead. My hands were burning up from the desire to write down the Fourteenth Tale, and there was not much time left either, before I would fail to fulfil the obligation of my vow. So, I asked my hosts for permission to leave. Mahmoud the Persian smiled and said, 'Name it- The Fourteenth Tale.'

The Mystery of the Miraculous Pomegranate

The Mystery of the Miraculous Pomegranate

1

Sheikh Dhākir has assigned me the duty of writing down this story and of copying it many times, and sending copies of it to other Muslim nations so that everyone will know how and under what circumstances we, the Shī'a of Bahrain, were able to get our reward for our love and devotion to the Imams ﷺ. The reason for this is so that everyone will know how we were saved from the great tribulation that we were subjected to.

It is also incumbent upon you, gentle readers, to relate this tale to others, so that news of this great incident will spread throughout the world, as this is the rightful desire of the Lord of the Age ﷺ. May these acts of ours be a handhold for our salvation on the Day of Judgment, God ﷻ willing.

The Mystery of the Miraculous Pomegranate

2

We Bahrainis[9] have a special place in our hearts for the Immaculate Imams ﷺ, and this is especially the case for the Imam who is in a state of occultation and who is therefore absent, i.e., the Lord of the Age ﷻ.

Woe to the rulers who have seized dominion over our lands and have ruled over them as hardened enemies of the Imams ﷺ, and who stop short of no form of oppression and inequity in their enmity towards us.

As I, Muḥammad the son of ʿĪsā (Jesus), am putting this tale in writing at the behest of Sheikh Dhākir, it is the 1,060th lunar year of the Islamic

---

[9] Bahrain is a Shīʿa-majority island nation off the coast of Arabia in the Persian Gulf that has been ruled by anti-Shīʿa rulers from 1783.

Calendar (1650 of the Christian Era). At this time, the sultan who rules over us has outdone his predecessors in his oppression and persecution of us, and worse than the sultan is his vizier or the person who ministers to all the sultan's affairs. It seems that the vizier can only take pleasure in persecuting us Shī'a, which sometimes takes an overt form, such as by levying heavy taxes on us, placing limits on our businesses and trade, and enacting other such iniquitous legislation. Sometimes, it would take a covert form, such as his setting fire to our orchards and fields, sinking our sea-faring vessels, or by spreading baseless, outrageous rumours and insults about our religious scholars and other notables within our community.

Our prayers always include the supplication that God ﷻ either rid us of the evil of this iniquitous ruler, or that He guide him to the right path, which is unlikely, of course, given the vehemence of his anti-Shī'a feelings and beliefs.

Last night, we heard that the sultan had invited the notables of Bahrain to his palace to show them a miracle that is supposed to have occurred. I, too, was among the invitees. A powerful anxiety came over me ever since the invitation reached me. My anxiety was so intense that it prevented my breakfast from being properly digested; it just sat there, weighing heavily on my stomach, as if I had swallowed a large stone. Nor did I eat any lunch, as I had no appetite for it, and I didn't want to subject my stomach to a repetition of the effect my breakfast had had on it.

As dusk approached, my wife Ra'ūf, may God ﷻ rest her soul, brought me some hot milk and a piece of bread and said, 'Eat this; it'll calm your stomach.'

'I have no appetite,' I replied.

She looked into my eyes and asked, 'What are you so worried about?'

I said, 'What is there *not* to be worried about when I know full well that the sultan and his minister, the vizier, are hatching up some plot against us again.'

Ra'ūf replied, 'What more can they possibly do? Really, I mean, how much worse can it get? The worst part of it is the divisions that they sow between the Shī'a and our Sunni brothers in faith. What *more* can they do?'

'May God ﷻ rid us of the evil of all evildoers,' I said.

I put a piece of bread in my mouth and washed it down with the hot milk that she had gone through the trouble of heating up for me, so that I wouldn't disappoint her. She gave me a sweet smile and left.

Ra'ūf was right. Most of the differences between us and our Sunni brethren are due to the evil machinations of our rulers. For example, Ra'ūf herself was originally Sunni. Still, even at that time, she had a great love for Her Eminence Lady Fāṭimah az-Zahrā' (the Luminous) ؑ. The reason for Ra'ūf's becoming Shī'a is a dream she had in which Lady Fāṭimah ؑ came to her and invited her to be her friend. That is when she decided to adopt the Shī'a *madhhab* or religio-legal rite.

Ra'ūf didn't have any problems up until the point when the sultan interfered and threatened her family. Her family and friends had accepted her conversion without any difficulty, but when the sultan took an interest and interfered with the situation, her family became sensitive to the issue, which caused her a lot of difficulties and anguish.

This situation continued until, to use Ra'ūf's words, I "rescued" her by asking for her hand in marriage, thereby relieving her of the pressures that were being brought to bear on her. After our marriage, her parents didn't come to visit her even once, for fear that her father's business dealings would be adversely affected.

Trust me, there are no depths that these sowers of the seeds of division will not stoop to. Their whole philosophy of governance is "divide and conquer." And that is precisely what they do: they sow the seeds of division so that they can reap the rewards of the disunity that ensues, and continue ruling in their own interests rather than in the interests of the community and nation as a whole.

The sun was getting ready to set when I heard a knock at my door. It was Sa'd, the son of Ḥasan, who had called on me in a distraught state of mind. His mind was so troubled and preoccupied that he had forgotten to greet me in his usual manner, which was for us to exchange kisses on each other's cheeks three times after offering our *salāms* to each other.

The Mystery of the Miraculous Pomegranate

He said, 'Let's go, Muḥammad. And may God ﷻ rid us of the evil of these wicked people.'

I replied, 'Come and have a cup of water, and run some over your face. It might make you feel better.'

He said, 'Hearing the news has left such a bitter taste in my mouth that I don't have an appetite for anything, even for water.'

I asked, 'What news?'

He said, 'Let's get going, and I'll tell you on the way.'

We said our farewells to Ra'ūf, who had become concerned about Saʻd's state, and started to head out. When we were leaving, she entrusted us to God's ﷻ care, and my last words to her were, 'Pray for us, Ra'ūf, as it seems some mischief is afoot.'

Once we were on our way, I asked Saʻd to tell me what was going on. He said, 'Haven't you heard the story of the Pomegranate?'

I said, 'Pomegranate? What Pomegranate?'

He stopped and turned towards me and said, 'What do you mean? You mean you haven't heard? The news of the pomegranate is everywhere.'

'I haven't left the house today,' I said, a little defensively.

He shook his head in reproach and said, 'Do you remember that stone that we found?'

'What stone?'

'You know, the one that had the names Ali, Ḥasan, and Ḥusain inscribed on it!' he said impatiently.

'Oh yeah, ok. Now I remember.'

'And what about the branch of that tree on which the name of our Master, the Lord of the Age, ﷺ could be seen to have appeared as a natural part of the growth of the branch, remember that?'

'Sure, I do. Who could forget it? So many people attained faith in the reality of the Lord of the Age ﷺ when they saw that.'

He said, 'OK. Well, now the vizier has found a pomegranate which has an inscription on it that, according to the sultan and his vizier, is a clear refutation of the Shī'a *madhhab*.'

'Come *on*,' I said, 'How's that even *possible*?!'

'I don't know. All I know is that I haven't ever seen Sheikh Dhākir so gloomy before.'

We had started walking again, and Sa'd took his strides at such a fast clip that I had a hard time keeping up with him. I grabbed his arm, and when he stopped, I stared him straight in his eyes and asked, 'What's written on the pomegranate?'

He shrugged and said, 'I don't know, but whatever it is, we're going to find out all about it tonight. God ﷻ only knows what mischief they have concocted up for us this time.' He then let out a sigh and said, 'As if our persecution wasn't enough, now they have to attack the veracity of our religion!'

When we got to Sheikh Dhākir's house, where a number of his friends and devotees had already gathered, the discussion that was taking place was along the same lines that Sa'd and I had been having. Everyone believed that what was afoot was nothing more than a lie and a trick to deceive the general public, and that there must be some secret behind the deception. None of us had any doubt about that whatsoever.

Sheikh Dhākir said with concern in his voice, 'The sultan and his vizier would never put themselves in a situation where we Shī'a could show them out as frauds, which is why I am very concerned that we will not be able to find a way out of the trap that they have laid down for us, in which case, God ﷻ help us!'

What the sheikh was saying was true, and we only realised the terrible truth of the matter when we saw the pomegranate with our own eyes. The sultan was dressed in formal attire and was reclining against the backrest of a low, carpeted platform. He had a smirk glued to his face from the very moment he saw us. The vizier was smiling and fully energised, going back and forth between one corner of the hall and another. It was evident that he couldn't contain the glee that he was holding within himself due to the "miracle" he was about to reveal.

The sultan eventually spoke, saying, 'Here is a sign and proof of the rightfulness and verity of the creed of our denomination (*madhhab*), which is at the same time a refutation of your creed. It is a true sign that the heart of nature itself has yielded to demonstrate to you how wayward you are and have

been and will remain if you continue on this same path.' Seeing the nod of the vizier's head that was the cue he was waiting for, a servant came forward holding a golden tray with both hands outstretched, in the middle of which the pomegranate rested. Sa'd squeezed my arm. I saw that all colour had left his face and that he had turned as pale as a ghost. Nor was I feeling any better than he was. All of the other guests who were

The Mystery of the Miraculous Pomegranate

Shī'a were similarly distraught. My hands and legs were quivering, especially at the moment when our sheikh picked up the pomegranate with an unsteady hand and stared at it in amazement.

The sheikh's amazement sent a wave of laughter through the hall, starting with the sultan himself, and then the vizier, followed by the obsequious courtiers in attendance who obediently followed suit. The sheikh had gone pale, and this only increased our anxieties. The pomegranate was passed from hand to hand until it got to me. I looked at it carefully and saw that the following inscription was embossed in the pomegranate's leathery skin in a line that formed a belt that girded the entirety of the circumference of the pomegranate:

> There is no deity other than Allāh,
> Muḥammad is the Apostle of Allāh,
> And Abū-Bakr, Umar, Uthmān, and Alī
> Are the Successors of the Apostle of Allāh.

I gave the pomegranate to Sa'd. When he read the inscriptions, he almost fainted. He quickly passed the pomegranate to the next person. I nudged his arm and said, 'Sa'd, don't for a moment think that this is anything other than a ruse.'

'Sure,' he replied, but it is a *massive* ruse!'

The sultan chuckled and said, 'I see that your amazement has you deep in thought, and that you are very concerned. And you have every right to be concerned. It wouldn't surprise me if throngs of people rejected your creed and left your ranks after seeing this miracle and joined those of us who are on the right path.' The sultan then turned to his vizier and said, 'They will no doubt rue the fact that they would be joining the right path so late in the game, eh?'

The vizier, whom I had never seen to be so happy, said, 'Indeed, sire.' He then turned to us and said, 'As you can see, this inscription cannot be the work of human hands, and it is nature herself who has decided to demonstrate the verity of the credo of our denomination over yours. Now, if there is even a smidgeon of integrity in any of you, you will not hesitate to put your stubbornness aside, reject your denomination and credo, and convert to the straight path.'

The pomegranate had made its way back to the sheikh, who was examining it with greater exactitude and care. The style of the writing on the pomegranate was beautiful in the extreme, and it seemed to me at the time that it was nature's intention to change our minds about our beliefs by way of the beauty of the script as well as by what it actually stated. Despondency and despair had penetrated into the very core of our beings. We looked to our sheikh to defend the rightfulness of our beliefs and to explain the reason for this unwelcome phenomenon, but suddenly the sheikh's hands lost their grip, and he almost dropped the pomegranate to the ground, but the alacrity and quick wit of one of the sultan's servants prevented this from happening by his being able to catch the pomegranate in midair. The sultan and the vizier jumped out of their seats in an automatic but futile attempt to prevent the pomegranate from falling to the ground, and breathed a sigh of relief when they saw that all was well with it and that it was safely nestled in the hands of one of the servants.

The vizier said in an indignant tone to the sultan, 'Did you see what they were doing? They wanted to destroy the pomegranate so that the manifest proof against their obstinacy would be destroyed! God only knows what other proofs of the verity of our faith have existed in the past that these people have done away with!'

The sheikh said, 'The truth of our faith has been proven without the need to resort to these kinds of "proofs," as you call them. It is in your heart, not ours, that such turmoil has been created as a consequence of some pomegranate.'

The sheikh's words bolstered all of our confidence and enabled us to snap out of our mesmerised incapacitation. The vizier said angrily, 'Prior to this blessed event, if you had a piece of wood or some such rot in which the names of your Imams were inscribed, you would show it to us and revel in their proving the supposed verity of your faith. But now that the tables have turned, why is it that you want to minimise the significance of this clear evidence?'

I said, 'Those signs were a point of pride for us, not a rational basis or proof for the rightfulness of our faith. There are so many rational and scriptural proofs in the Quran and in our hadith reports for the rightfulness of the claims of our Imams ﷺ that we do not see a need to resort to these kinds of reasons.'

The sheikh gave me an approving look and a nod, and I saw from the whispered approvals and nods of my companions that what I had said was appropriate. The vizier looked at me angrily and was preparing to respond to what I had said when the sultan raised his hand and said, 'Enough! This discussion is at an end!' He then pointed an accusatory finger in our direction and said, 'The vizier is right. The inscription on this pomegranate is the most perfect and most beautiful natural proof that has been seen by human eyes to date, and it unquestionably proves and affirms the verity and rightfulness of *our* faith. Therefore, from this point forward, you will be no different to us than non-Muslim infidels!'

When the sultan had made this terrible statement of mass excommunication and anathemization, the phrase "God forbid" rose from the crowd, and a number of people groaned and could be seen striking themselves on their heads in desperation.

Dāwūd yelled, 'What kind of believers *are* you, who can equate your brothers in faith with non-Muslim unbelievers?!'

The vizier picked up the pomegranate, held it before our eyes, and said, 'That is very simple! It has to do with the moral imperative and ordinances having to do with the moral stewardship of the community (*aḥkām -e nezāratī*), such as *amr bil ma'rūf wa nahī 'anil munkar*, which is a pillar of the religion and which refers to the imperative to enjoin the doing of that which is right and to forbid the doing of that which is wrong! Now; we have demonstrated the path of truth to you by way of this manifest miraculous sign, and it is up to you to choose either to join our creed and rite (*madhhab*) and garner its rewards from God ﷻ in this world and in the world to come, or to persist in your own creed and rite, in which case the sultan will decide your fate.'

The sultan nodded his head vigorously in affirmation and said, 'Indeed! Either convert to Sunni Islam like everyone else, in which case you will be the beneficiary of our grace as well as that of God's ﷻ; or, accept the superiority of our religion and pay tribute (*jizya*)[10] to the government like the Christians and Jews. Or...'

At this point, the sultan broke off and smiled, then continued in a tone that betrayed that he was giving a third option that was impossible to fulfil, saying, 'Or bring forward a strong reason for the rejection of the proof provided by this pomegranate and the precious guiding words that are inscribed on it.'

The vizier laughed aloud and shook his head in affirmation of the sultan's tone, which implied the

---

[10] *Jizya*: a tax levied on non-Muslim citizens of the Muslim state in exchange for the protection they receive and in lieu of the taxes, such as *zakāt*, that only Muslims pay.

impossibility of such a task. The sultan said, 'And if you do not accept either one of these two options, we will slaughter your menfolk, and take your womenfolk and children captive as slaves, and will also seize and confiscate your property.'

Sheikh Dhākir shook his head and said, 'This is patent injustice and outright persecution.'

And the sultan replied, 'To the contrary; it is the embodiment of justice itself!'

I said, 'What justice? You place such a great divide between Sunnis and Shī'a, and act as if we are not brothers in the same religion!'

Sa'd added, 'How dare you make such a ruling as this against us?!'

This riled the sultan's ire, who stood up from his seat and said, 'Stop these useless arguments at once! And decide immediately, as I want to execute my order.'

Sheikh Dhākir raised his hands and said, 'Then give us the opportunity to discuss the decision that we must take with each other before we can come to our decision.'

The sultan looked over at his vizier. It seemed he needed his vizier's approval to respond to the sheikh.

The vizier said, 'Very well! We are certain of what your decision will be, and of the sultan's command; but we will give you three days to consult with each other so that later, your long tongues won't wag to say that the sultan did not act justly.' He then bowed deeply to the sultan and said, 'That is, if the sultan agrees with this dispensation, of course.'

For his part, the sultan said, 'The vizier's ruling shall stand. You have three days to think this through, but I hope that you will decide wisely and make a decision that will be in your own interests.'

I wanted to issue a protest, but remained silent at the sheikh's behest, who had realised the futility of any such remonstration.

We exited the sultan's palace in a mood of complete dejection. I had never felt so humiliated in my whole life. My companions felt the same way. You could see the condition of their souls written across their faces. Our sheikh stood in our midst and said, 'The vizier's intention is to create division between the Muslims. It is his usual mode of operation: divide and conquer.'

I said, 'I agree,' and this was followed by a buzz in the crowd to the same effect.

The sheikh said, 'Instead of falling into their evil trap, we need to try to find a way to prevent the division that has been sown between the Muslims from getting any deeper.'

'So, what should we do?' I asked.

The sheikh placed a hand on my shoulder and said, 'We have to take refuge in God ﷻ, my son, and entrust our affairs to Him.'

He then started to walk among the crowd, and with a sweet smile on his face, told us that ultimately, we would prevail. He closed by saying, 'Now go back home and reassure your families that everything will be all right. I will wait for you in the congregational mosque.'

I don't know how I got myself back home. I was so lost in my thoughts that I managed to regain the normal consciousness of what I was doing and where I was going only after I was standing in front of my own house. As soon as I was about to knock on the door, it was opened, revealing the distraught face of Ra'ūf standing behind the threshold. I said, 'Hey, lady of the house, do you then open the door to anyone who knocks on it without asking who it is?'

'After all these years, I know the sound of your walk,' she said.

She moved to the side, and I entered our house's courtyard. I smelled the welcome fragrance of fresh-baked bread, and I smelled moist earth.

The Mystery of the Miraculous Pomegranate

The Mystery of the Miraculous Pomegranate

When I sat on the low platform that was situated under a great grapevine, I felt a certain peace and tranquillity under the intermittent shade of the vine's leaves, but the feeling was accompanied by a sense that the serenity wouldn't last and would soon be lost. This other sense ultimately became dominant and engendered a whole host of pent-up emotions in me that I could not contain. I thought, 'Will all this go up in flames as a result of the unjust dictates of a tyrant?' Ra'ūf was washing some grapes and preparing to bring me a plate of them. I thought about who Ra'ūf and the boy or girl that she was carrying in her womb would become slaves to. Suddenly, the prospect of their enslavement brought up a great fear and sent a shiver up my spine.

I hid my face with my hands and wept silently. I then heard the sound of the plate of grapes falling to the ground and breaking, and the sound of Ra'ūf moaning and pleading, through the right of the Imams ﷺ and the Daughter of the Prophet, to tell her what happened and what kind of trouble we were facing.

I splashed some water on my face from the little pool we had in our courtyard and then went and sat next to Ra'ūf. She was clawing at her cheeks and was in obvious agony. I told her, 'It is better that you don't know what happened. It would do you no good, nor would it be any good for our little baby, which you are carrying.'

She let out a sigh and said, 'I'll suffer even more if I don't know. I swore to you by the rank the Imams ﷺ have with God ﷻ to tell me what happened.'

I had no choice but to tell her what happened, but I did so by leaving out some of the worst parts so that she would not panic. She was feeling very vulnerable after I had finished telling her what had taken place. Her reaction was to say, 'So what is the worst they can do to us that they haven't already done? If our baby comes into the world and cannot be raised as a Shi'ā, then it would be better if it weren't born at all!'

After she said this, she fell silent. The words of our sheikh reverberated in my mind, which prompted me to say, 'Then where has your faith gone, and your trust in God ﷻ ? All of us are supposed to meet up in the mosque. We will stay there and take counsel with each other until we find a solution. Don't worry! God ﷻ will rid us of the evil of these wicked people.'

She asked, 'What about us women and children, what are we supposed to do?'

I said, 'You know better than I do what you need to do. You are one of the chosen of Lady Fāṭimah ﷺ; pray to her and ask her to guide us, just as she came to you in your dream and guided you.'

She bit her lip and nodded as a tear rolled down her cheek. I had no more time to tarry around. I heard a knock at the door and knew it was Sa'd. I got up and said 'Pray for us' in lieu of a farewell.

Sa'd and I took off. It was evident from the redness of his eyes that, like me, Sa'd had been weeping. He was holding a lantern whose light shivered on the wall of my house, betraying the unsteadiness of the hand that was holding the lantern.

We had not gone far when I heard the door to our house open. I looked back and saw Ra'ūf, who was standing just outside the door, looking at us. I waved at her and gave her a reassuring smile, then turned back and prayed for God ﷻ to keep her safe, her and the little one she was carrying inside her womb.

The Mystery of the Miraculous Pomegranate

4

I was looking up, staring at the arched brickwork that formed the dome of the mosque. The sound of the discussions and occasional arguments that were taking place reverberated in the dome and echoed back down. The light of the lanterns quivered on the ceiling. I closed my eyes and listened to the sounds. Hāmid's voice was the loudest. He was saying, '... This is the ruling of the sacred law. We will ostensibly convert to their *madhhab* but will maintain our love for Imam Ali ﷺ and [for the purified and immaculate members of] his family ﷺ and will follow the rulings of our own *madhhab* when it comes to our rites of worship and ritual devotions. This will ensure that the conspiracy of the sultan and his vizier to kill us and steal our property, or to treat us as non-Muslims who pay tribute, will come to naught.'

A few people affirmed Hāmid's position, saying that they agreed with him. I opened my eyes and looked at Sheikh Dhākir. He was frowning, and I knew that he did not agree with Hāmid's approach.

He said, 'What could be a worse humiliation than for us to set aside our faith, which is the one true faith, in order to save our lives and property?'

Hāmid said, 'As I said, Sheikh, we would only do this ostensibly as a form of *taqīyyah* (prudential dissimulation) and would remain true to our faith inwardly.'

Saʻd slapped his hand on his thigh and said, 'But what *possible* good could come out of that, brother? We might have saved our own skins by doing that, but if the news of what we are doing gets out – and it is bound to get out – do you know what will happen? Woe to us if we give up on a faith that our forefathers made great sacrifices in blood and treasure for, simply for the filthy lucre of this world.'

Hāmid replied, 'What you say is all well and good, but what other solution *is* there? Paying tribute as non-Muslims is even worse. I'm prepared to die and have my property looted, but not be subjected to the humiliation of being treated as a non-Muslim.'

I said, 'Well, that is precisely why we have all gathered here this evening, dear Hāmid. We have to find a solution that enables us to maintain our faith, which precludes us from paying any sort of non-

Muslim tribute and does not put our own lives and the lives of our families at risk.'

I thought of Ra'ūf and the fear that I saw in her eyes, and I thought of the child she was carrying, whom we had decided to name Mahdī if he were a boy, and Fāṭimah if she were a girl. A lump of pent-up emotions formed in my throat, and I closed my eyes to prevent my tears from spilling over.

I heard the sheikh's voice saying, 'Muḥammad is right. Ultimately, the solution is to put the lie to the so-called "miracle" of the pomegranate.'

Saʿd said, 'But how is that possible? The inscription on that pomegranate is very precise and clear, and it is undeniable.'

I had thought to name our child Mahdī if he were to be a boy, as he had been the subject of the special attention of our master, the Lord of the Age ﷻ, and for whom we had been waiting in anticipation for years. Ra'ūf and I made intercessory recourse (*tawassul*) with the Lord of the Age ﷻ, asking him to intercede on our behalf with God ﷻ. We had vowed that if God ﷻ were to grant us a child, we would raise him as one who would be a servant of the Ahl al-Bayt (the Purified and Immaculate members of the House of the Prophet) ﷺ, be it a boy or a girl. Then, suddenly, the thought occurred to me: Why not make intercessory recourse with the Lord of the Age ﷻ?

I said with much excitement, 'Brothers, why not ask the Lord of the Age ﷻ to come to our aid?'

Everyone started talking about my idea. Hāmid asked, 'How would we do that, specifically?'

I said, 'Well, we all know that there is something fishy about that pomegranate and that it is not a real reason or proof of what they claim it is. The truth of our faith tells us that much, and *that* we are sure of. Therefore, there must be some mystery behind the creation of that pomegranate that has to be revealed, and this secret cannot be revealed other than by supernatural means. Let us place our trust in God ﷻ and make intercessory recourse (*tawassul*) with the Lord of the Age ﷺ, asking him to intercede on our behalf and reveal the secret of this mystery to us.'

Sheikh Dhākir let out a sigh of relief and said, '*Aḥsant!* Well said! May God ﷻ reward you, Muḥammad, for you always come up with the ultimate and best solutions.' He then turned to the crowd and said, 'We already know that Muḥammad has supplicated to the Lord of the Age ﷺ, and that his wife is expectant as a result!'

Tears started to well up in my eyes. I said, 'As God ﷻ is my witness, we had tried everything and nothing had worked, and we were in the nadir of despair when we made intercessory recourse with the Imam ﷺ. My supplicatory ritual devotions had not reached their fortieth night when His Eminence came to me in a dream, gave me a sprig of jasmine flowers, and said, "Smell the fragrance of your child." So, who could be better than him? Who else could save us from the nightmare of this tyrant and the wicked machinations of his evil vizier?'

Sa'd put his arm around Hāmid's shoulders and said, 'Don't blame yourself, brother. We were *all* at fault for not having thought of taking recourse with the Lord of the Age ﷻ sooner.' He then turned to me and said, 'And bravo to you, Muḥammad, for suggesting the best of solutions.'

I lowered my head and said, 'I'm sure that if the thought hadn't occurred to me, it would have occurred to someone else. Now what we have to decide on is how to connect with the Master ﷻ.'

Everyone's head turned towards our sheikh, as the decision ultimately lay in his hands. He said, 'We will proceed in the same way that has happened in the past, in which His Eminence appeared before those who are in need, most of whom were alone and saw him on their own. The people to whom he appeared were renowned for their faith and piety and for their sincerity. We have been given three nights, so we will choose three people who are the most preeminent among us in terms of their faith, piety and sincerity. Each of these will be assigned to go out into the wilderness and ask to see the Imam ﷺ. If the first of these sees the Imam ﷺ, then all will be well, and we will praise God ﷻ. But if not, then the second one will go out, and if he does not meet with success, then the third one will try.'

I said, 'I am certain that the Imam ﷺ will come. Now let us see who among us is worthy of being in his presence.'

Each and every one of Bahrain's notables had lived a life of piety and was renowned for their moral rectitude, but we chose the most pious among us with the help of our sheikh's counsel. There ended up being nine people, and no matter how much we insisted, the sheikh did not consent to be the tenth. He would say things like, 'We would lose our chance, because there are others who are worthier than me,' which, of course, was not the case. For the tenth person, Sheikh Dhākir raised his hand and said, 'For the tenth person, I nominate Muḥammad the son of 'Īsā.'

I said, 'Sheikh! How can you nominate an unworthy sinner such as myself to join a group in which even you yourself are not a part of??'

'Upon my word with God ﷻ, I know that you spend more time on the [supererogatory] nighttime ritual devotions and supplications than I do. I have neither heard a single lie from you, nor have I ever heard you talking behind anyone's back, and I know that you haven't cheated anyone out of even a single dinar's worth of their rights. I also know that you perform all of your religious obligations to the letter of the law; and it is you, not us, who have already had the honour of seeing His Eminence's countenance.'

I lowered my head, and a shiver ran through my body. What if the sheikh chooses me as one of the final three? Ultimately, the ten people were narrowed down to three. Ali, the son of Sharīf, was the first, whom, despite his denials, everyone swore to his piety and to the soundness of his character. Saʻd, the son of Ḥasan, was the second person, and he kept on saying, 'Don't ruin your chances by choosing me. There are those who are more pious than I among you. Please do not place this burden on my shoulders.'

The sheikh then smiled at me in a way that let me know that the third person was to be none other than me. I wanted to object, but the sheikh turned to the rest of the group and asked, 'Do you agree with my nomination of Muḥammad, the son of ʻĪsā?' To which the group agreed unanimously, each of the members of which started to sing the praises of my character!

I said, 'I feared nothing more than being selected as one of our three representatives. God ﷻ willing, Saʻd or Ali will succeed so that my turn will never come, because I know they are worthier than I am.'

The sheikh said, 'God ﷻ knows best! So then, as we discussed earlier, let Ali go forth and supplicate the Imam ؑ to appear. If he does not succeed, Saʻd will go next, and if *he* does not succeed, it will be up to Muḥammad to save us on the third and final night.'

I had not yet left the mosque when its custodian called out to me and pointed my attention to a corner of the mosque's courtyard in which a woman was standing holding a lantern with an unsteady hand.

The custodian said, 'It seems your wife is here.'

I went to her and said, 'Ra'ūf, what are you doing here? It's past midnight!'

She hurried towards me and said, 'I couldn't stand it any longer. I needed to tell you something that couldn't wait.'

'What is it that's so urgent?'

'I wanted to say, why not ask our hidden Imam ﷻ to help us?'

I said, 'That is exactly what we have decided to do, dear. We have decided to ask him to come and guide us out of the dilemma that we face.'

She breathed a sigh of relief and praised God ﷻ. '*Alḥamdulillāh*,' she said.

We started on our way back home under the shaky lights given off by the lanterns, and on the way back, I told her all about what had taken place in the mosque. No matter how I tried, I was unable to bring myself to tell her that I was also chosen as one of the final three candidates. I silently prayed to God ﷻ to make it so that this heavy responsibility would be concluded with the Imam's appearance before one or the other of the first two candidates. I was walking a step or two ahead of Ra'ūf, but I could still feel that there was something wrong with her. She dragged her feet on the ground and let out the occasional sigh. I asked, 'Are you not feeling well?'

She said with a quiver in her voice, 'No, not really. I was so anxious this evening to see what would be decided, and that anxiousness still hasn't left me.'

I said, 'Do you want me to take you to see Umm Ya'qūb?'

She held my hand and started walking, saying, 'No, not now. I'll be alright. There's still another month to go before my due date. You know how Umm Ya'qūb is; as soon as she sees me, she'll start grumbling about how I'm not looking after myself, and how I'll damage the baby if I carry on like this, and how she won't be my midwife anymore – you know how she is...'

I smiled. Ra'ūf was so adept at making me feel better. I was still concerned, but her words had taken the edge off my worries.

When we entered our home, I saw that every corner of the house was full of light. I said without thinking, 'Why have you lit every lantern in the house?' Then I regretted my question, as I realised that she must have been scared. But Ra'ūf removed her *chādor*,[11] smiled, and said, 'I knew that you would want to pray more than your usual supererogatory prayers, and that you would probably be praying until the middle of the night tonight, so I filled the house with light so that you wouldn't be praying in the dark.'

That brought a big smile to my face. I said, 'Truly, you are one who is guided by Lady Fāṭimah ﷺ. May God ﷻ bless your heart. The light of your faith and wisdom is sufficient for me. I can perform my prayers

---

[11] A *chādor* is a full body-length cloth that is worn over a woman's head, and which comes down to the ankles. It is open in front but is held closed with the hands.

and supplications with the light of a single lantern too, of course. But thank you for thinking of me and doing this. It is special. And yes, I think that I will be staying up all night tonight, as I don't think I'll be able to sleep.'

As she was laying down my prayer mat, she said, 'I will stay up with you. She then got up with an effort, and I said, 'I don't think that is what God ﷻ would want, my dear, with you being in the condition you are in. Think of the baby and go and get some sleep.'

Ra'ūf lowered her head and went into the other room. I extinguished the wicks of all but one of the lanterns, and as I was making my ritual ablutions, I looked heavenward. Dark clouds obscured my view of the stars and the moon. I thought to myself, 'If only I could at least see the moon tonight,' and then I thought of the luminous visage of the Lord of the Age ﷻ, which shone as brightly as the moon. And then I thought, 'Is it really possible for me to see him one more time?'

I spent that whole night in prayer and supplication. Ra'ūf continually let out moans in her sleep and woke up in the morning with a pale face that was drained of all signs of life. I became very concerned for her and decided to remain at home to be by her side, and did not venture out to the mosque. I persisted in wanting to take her to see Umm Ya'qūb, but she demurred. She said, 'Don't worry about me. Now is not the right time for that. Now is the time for making prayers and supplications. Don't neglect that. I'm fine.'

She moved around with difficulty, but she still managed to invoke God's ﷻ blessings (*dhikr*) for us using her clay *tasbīḥ* (the Muslim form of the rosary).

She started feeling a little better a little after noon. The hours passed, and just as I was making my ritual ablutions at dusk for the evening prayers, Sa'd came after me, saying, 'Why didn't you come to the mosque for the morning and noon prayers? The *masjid* (mosque) was packed.'

I said, 'Ra'ūf wasn't feeling well; I couldn't leave her alone.'

'How about now? Is she feeling better? We're supposed to accompany Ali halfway out to the wilderness and pray for his success. If you want, we can swing by Umm Ya'qūb's place and have her stop by to check on Ra'ūf.'

I agreed to the plan and let Ra'ūf know what we were up to. She said, 'But I don't want you to go out of your way on my account. Go and tell Ali that all of the women and children are praying for his success.'

Sa'd and I left the house and had only taken a few steps towards Umm Ya'qūb's house when we saw her turn the corner from the main street into our alley. I went forward and, after greeting her, said, 'Umm Ya'qūb, we were just heading over to see you!'

Umm Ya'qūb cast a glance at Sa'd and I, and said with a certain sadness in her eyes, 'So it's on the shoulders of you two and Ali, the son of Sharīf, to save the Shī'a of Bahrain?'

I said, 'We are just doing what the community thinks best. We have placed our trust in God ﷻ and are making *tawassul* (intercessory recourse) with the Lord of the Age ﷻ.'

She nodded and said, 'May God ﷻ be with you. I was worried about Ra'ūf, so I thought I'd stop by.'

I said, 'As a matter of fact, she is not feeling well. I'm concerned about her, too. Can you be with her for the next two or three days while we are busy with this other business? You know how her parents...'

She nodded and said, 'Yeah, I know all about that. Don't worry. I'll make sure she's ok.'

We left her, with my heart being much more assured knowing that Ra'ūf would be in good hands, and met up with Ali, whose bloodshot eyes betrayed the fact that he had been up all night weeping in supplication. When I embraced him, I noticed that his body was shaking, and his breath smelled like he had not had food in a long while. His face was pale, and it was evident that he was fasting.

It had grown dark, and our lanterns only lit the area immediately around us. Some of the womenfolk had shown up too, bringing their children with them, and they started wailing as soon as we left Ali to venture out the rest of the way into the wilderness on his own. Ali looked so pitiable with his slouched shoulders and the way he dragged his feet as he walked. My heart went out to him.

I don't know why, but as soon as the last of the light of Ali's lantern could no longer be seen in the

darkness, all of the womenfolk cried out. We prayed the Faraj[12] prayer at Sheikh Dhākir's prompting by way of a send-off for Ali. Although I knew that Umm Ya'qūb was with Ra'ūf and that she was in good hands, my heart was still filled with anxiety and worry. My mind was divided between concern for Ali on one hand, and concern for Ra'ūf on the other. I couldn't sit still, and constantly got up and walked around. Eventually, Sheikh Dhākir came up to me and said, 'Relax a little, Muḥammad. Sit and read the Qur`ān for a while; that'll calm you down.'

I said, 'I can't concentrate. But I'll try.' I sat and started reading the Qur`ān, and I read and read some more, and I was taken over by the magnetic effect of the verses of our sacred book. I only came back to my normal state of mind when the white thread of dawn

---

[12] Relief; A prayer for the rising of the 12th Imam.

was becoming visible in the night sky, and people had started to wake up to perform the morning prayer, looking anxiously in the direction where Ali had disappeared into the wilderness.

When everyone had awakened and had made their ritual ablutions and taken their positions to perform the congregational morning prayers, Sheikh Dhākir took the position of prayer leader, and we performed two extended cycles of the morning ritual devotions on the periphery of the wilderness, which was accompanied by much weeping. We were in the middle of our supplications when we saw Ali appear in the distance with his shoulders slouched over. He did not need to say anything to us to realise that his supplications had not met with success. When he came closer and we could see his face, it seemed as if he had aged several years overnight. He knelt at Sheikh Dhākir's feet, dried his eyes with the hem of the sheikh's robe, and said, 'He didn't come, Sheikh... He didn't come. What will we do if he doesn't appear?'

That sent everyone into a delirium of weeping and wailing. The womenfolk cried out the loudest. I bent down and kissed the Qur'ān, and a shiver of anxiety ran up my spine. What would happen to Ra'ūf? What would be the fate of our unborn child?

Sheikh Dhākir stood on a boulder and said, 'Don't lose hope, people. We chose three people, not one, and there was a good reason for that. Upon my word of honour before God ﷻ, I have never heard of an instance where someone has sincerely and with all of his being asked the Lord of the Age ﷺ for his help, who has not been helped by him. So be patient and persevere, and God ﷻ willing, tonight will be the night when we will be guided to the truth. We will offer the Ḥājāt (requests) supplication today in the *masjid* and will recite the Faraj *du'ā'* (supplication) until evening.'

Sa'd laid a hand on my arm and said in a plaintive voice, 'If only you had not chosen me.'

'It's a religiously incumbent duty, Sa'd,' I replied, 'Who could we have chosen who would have been worthier than you?'

He said, 'Please don't say that. *Anyone* would have been better than me.' He then paused for a moment, then said, 'Let me tell you something, and I will tell it only to you and to no one else. If I head out to the wilderness tonight and do not see the Imam, I will not return. How could I? How could I look anyone in the eyes after that?'

His pent-up emotions had formed a lump in his throat that prevented him from being able to say anything else, and tears started to run down his cheeks.

I said, 'We'll go to the *masjid*, recite prayers and supplications, and entrust our affairs to God ﷻ. God ﷻ is greater than all of our trials and tribulations.'

I felt so sorry for him that I couldn't leave him to be on his own. Each person we passed said something different, but they were all in the vein of things like, 'You are our hope, Sa'd,' and 'We're counting on you, Sa'd,' and so on.

I knew the kind of fire that these words lit in Sa'd's heart. I was aware that he knew I was feeling the same way, which is why he had grabbed hold of my arm and wouldn't let it go. I accompanied him to the *masjid* and left him there so that I could run back home to see how Ra'ūf was doing and then head back to the *masjid*. I asked Sheikh Dhākir for permission to leave and then headed out. I came across a number of people on the way home who were part of the sultan's entourage. Their mockery and snide remarks felt like a dagger was being stabbed into my heart. They said things like, 'They have become desperate... whoever heard of taking recourse in an Imam that no one has seen head or tail of? How stupid! ... Desperados...'

I silently prayed, 'O Lord, on the right that Your Apostle ﷺ has with You, don't let the devotees of Your Apostle's House ﷺ be humiliated.'

When I got home, Umm Ya'qūb opened the door. The bruising around her eyes told me that she had been up all night, too.

'How is she doing?' I asked, after greeting her.

Without replying to my question, she asked, 'What happened? Did Ali succeed in seeing the Imam ﷻ?'

I shook my head. Umm Ya'qūb's eyes filled with tears. I looked in on Ra'ūf, who was asleep. Her head was drenched in sweat, and the skin all around her eyes was dark with bruising. Umm Ya'qūb said, 'She's just been able to fall asleep. There's still a way to go before her final month is up. The baby hasn't rotated yet. But she is feeling labour pangs already.'

I asked, 'What does that mean? What's going to happen now?'

Umm Ya'qūb said, 'I don't know. May God ﷻ have mercy on the two of you, for you have been waiting so long to have a child.'

That made me so concerned. I thought about the Lord of the Age ﷺ and whether he would take back what he had given.

I went back to the bedroom to check up on Ra'ūf again. I wanted to call her name and talk to her and comfort her, but Umm Ya'qūb stopped me, telling me that it would be better to let her get the sleep she needs. She then said, 'Actually, she missed you a lot. Can't you stay until she wakes up?'

I didn't know what to say or do. I was torn between two important responsibilities, but ultimately decided that I had better get back to the mosque. So, I said, 'I'll try to come back later or send someone to make sure everything is alright. And if something comes up, let me know.'

Umm Ya'qūb took a peek at Ra'ūf, nodded, and said, 'God ﷻ bless your mother's soul. Your responsibilities are much heavier than mine. I wish that there was something that I could do to help.'

I couldn't stay any longer. I told her that what she was doing was already a great help, said my goodbyes, and left.

The Mystery of the Miraculous Pomegranate

We saw Saʻd off that night, just as we had sent Ali off into the wilderness the night before. Some of the members of our group were exhausted from their lack of sleep. Sheikh Dhākir said a prayer. The sky was cloudless, but for some reason, there were very few stars visible; it was as if they had been covered by a veil of dust or by some other occlusion. I sat down and leaned back against a tree. I was feeling dejected. 'O Lord,' I thought, what kind of test is this that has torn my heart and mind in two?' At one moment, my thoughts were on the conspiracy of the vizier, and at another, they skipped to Ra'ūf's condition. These were the thoughts my mind was occupied with when I fell into a deep sleep and woke up with the sound of Sheikh Dhākir reciting the *adhān* (call to prayer).

Everyone had already made their ritual ablutions and were standing in line, ready to start the congregational prayer. I was upset with myself for having slept for a few hours instead of spending them in prayer, supplication, and Qur'ānic recitation, as we had all committed to do. I rushed towards Sheikh Dhākir, pleading with him, 'Upon my honour, send someone else who is worthy! A person such as myself, who falls asleep as soon as he closes his eyes, and who cannot even stay up for two nights to offer prayers and make supplications to the Lord of the Age ﷻ, is not worthy of being sent into the wilderness so that he might perchance appear before me!'

Sheikh Dhākir looked into my eyes with such vehemence that it sent a shiver up my spine. He said calmly, 'O Muḥammad, there is something within your character that is rarely seen in others. Upon my word of honour with God ﷻ, I would not have you change your place with anyone, even if it meant having my head severed from my body!'

I bowed down low to kiss his hands, but he pulled his hands away and wouldn't let me. He said, 'Come, my son. The people are waiting. Come and let us pray together.'

There was such passion in Sheikh Dhākir's voice that it brought tears to my eyes, and it was all I could do to prevent them from flowing down my cheeks, which they eventually did anyway. My shoulders convulsed as I wept, while at the same time I recited the Qur'ānic verses that the prayers consisted of. It was only while my consciousness was in the moment of making these two cycles of ritual devotions that my mind was neither on my concern for the Shī'a community of which I was a part, nor even on my concern for Ra'ūf and what would happen to her and her childbirth. My mind was only on God ﷻ, and His presence had illuminated my heart to such an extent that a strange sense of calm had overcome me and all my anxieties.

The Mystery of the Miraculous Pomegranate

6

The sun dawned on the morning of the next day, but there was still no sign of Sa'd. We were all very concerned. I suddenly remembered what he had said about not returning if the Imam ﷺ didn't appear to him.

I said to Sheikh Dhākir, 'He's not going to show up, Sheikh. The Imam ﷺ has not appeared to him, and he feels too ashamed to show his face.'

Sheikh Dhākir ran his hand over his face and beard and said, 'Let's head out there! We have to find him.'

So, we set off. It didn't take long for us to find him. He was sitting on top of a hill, not too far away from where we had left him. I ran to him and shook him gently. I held his head to my chest and called out his name. He said in a weak, trembling voice, 'Is that you, Muḥammad? I couldn't even pray... I wasn't able to do anything! I just sat here and stared at the distance over there. Now it's your turn to try to save us!'

He then rested his head on my shoulder and wept, triggering everyone else to do the same. Even Sheikh Dhākir turned away from us and wiped the tears from his cheeks. I kissed Saʿd on the crown of his head and said, 'The fact that the Imam ﷺ didn't appear to you is not an indication of your lack of faith. Entrust your affairs to God ﷻ as I do, and to no one else.'

I helped Saʿd get back home, as he didn't have enough energy or even the will to get there by himself. Sheikh Dhākir said, 'I know you are worried about your wife. Go and check up on her and make sure everything is ok. I'll see you at the *masjid*. We'll offer our prayers again and make more supplications, in the hope that some opening will occur the third time around.'

I couldn't see any sign of the worry that everyone else was obviously feeling on the Sheikh's face. There was a frown on his face, to be sure, but he was not fretting.

Our house was full of women when I got there. When they saw me, some of them started to cry. I thought to myself that Ra'ūf must have passed away.

Umm Yaʿqūb came forward and yelled at the women, 'What on Earth is the matter with all of you?! Do you want to give him a heart attack? Is that it?' She then took me by the sleeve to the bedroom.

I said, 'Umm Ya'qūb, tell me what has happened to her!'

She said, 'Nothing! So far, she is fine. She is feeling a lot of birth pangs, but the child refuses to budge. I don't know what to do.'

'Has the baby died?' I asked.

'No,' she said. 'The poor little thing is still moving but won't come out. Pray for her.' And then it seemed that she remembered the date that I had in the wilderness tonight, and she added, 'May God ﷻ be with you, my son.'

The woman in the room didn't look anything like the Ra'ūf that I knew. She was very gaunt and decrepit, with deep-set eyes in her face that had turned tawny. I sat next to her and called out her name. She didn't respond to my calls until one of my tears fell on her hand. She closed her hand and opened her eyes. When she saw me, she forced a smile onto her face and, in a very soft voice, said, 'Forgive me,' as if she was asking for me to forgive any trespass she might have committed against me, so that her conscience would be clear before she went from this world to the next.

I said, 'What kind of thing is that to say, Ra'ūf? I have seen nothing but goodness and kindness from you. Besides, I am certain in my heart of hearts that you and our baby will be fine.'

'Will you be going out into the wilderness tonight?'

I knew what she meant and knew the answer she expected to hear, and nodded my affirmation. She smiled and said, 'If you had said that you were not going, that you were going to stay by my side, I wouldn't have looked at you ever again.'

Upon my word, nothing she could have said made me happier than the words that she had just uttered. I entrusted her to God's ﷻ care and set out to make my way back to the mosque.

The atmosphere in the mosque was different and strange. People could be heard weeping and wailing. Sheikh Dhākir was sitting in a corner. When I entered, everyone stood up in my honour, as if I were some high dignitary or something. I felt so ashamed that I sat down immediately right to the side of the door I'd just entered so that everyone else would sit back down too, and insisted that they not embarrass me like they had just done by standing up at my entrance. Sheikh Dhākir came over, took hold of my hands, lifted me to my feet, and walked me to the middle of the gathering and told someone, 'Bring some bread and a few dates.' When the bread and dates were given to him, he placed them in front of me and said, 'Do you realise how long it's been since you've had anything to eat? I'm sure that you didn't eat anything at home either.'

'I have no appetite,' I replied.

He said, 'The bread is blessed (*tabarruk*[13]); it has come to us from the shrine of our Master, Imam Ḥusain

---

[13] *Tabarruk*: the property of a relic or some mundane object which is believed to have been blessed or charged in some other way with sacral properties.

The Mystery of the Miraculous Pomegranate

ﷺ. Now eat it so you can gain your strength back, as you have a very arduous night ahead of you.'

The mention of the night that I had before me sent a quiver through my heart and made me break out in a cold sweat. Yes, I indeed faced an arduous night, as did my wife too.

Bread and dates had never tasted so good. I must have been very hungry, or perhaps it was because the bread had been charged with blessings; I don't know. In any case, it hit the spot, gave me energy, and revived my spirit. We spent the rest of the day praying and supplicating. After we made the evening prayers, everyone got up to accompany me to the same place as we had all gone to on the previous two nights, from which point I was to make the rest of the way on my own into the wilderness. I said to my comrades, 'I beseech you not to trouble yourselves to come out with me all that way. Allow me to forget your concerns and to forget the worried looks that I see on your faces now. Leave me to myself so that I can make my own way into the wilderness and make my supplications without being worried about your anxieties.'

Ḥāmid said, 'Don't you want to be charged and inspired by our presence and support?'

I said, 'You are all better than me; it is only because of my love and respect for all of you that I ask that you not accompany me and not wait up for me. Allow my mind to be free from worrying about my comrades staying up all night in anticipation of what will happen, so that I can focus my prayers and supplications with a greater peace of mind.'

I kissed Sheikh Dhākir's shoulders and said, 'Pray for me.'

Sheikh Dhākir said, 'And we would have you pray for us.'

There was a special sparkle in the sheikh's eyes, as if he was aware of some secret that nobody else knew. I bid farewell to everyone and started off on my short journey, without taking a lantern with me. I took a different route, because I knew that people were anticipating the path I was expected to take and were waiting for me to show up so that they could accompany me to the departure point. Every Shī'a citizen of the small island state of Bahrain could not eat or sleep properly that night, as they all burned with the intensity of their anticipation of what their destiny would be.

I took back roads and passed by deserted alleys and byways. The smell of baked bread fresh out of clay ovens, the scent of moist soil and the light of lanterns being emitted out of the houses I passed reminded me of my own house and of the woman who had experienced much strife in her life. She could be undergoing her most arduous test right now, which might involve losing the infant whose arrival we had been anticipating for so long. What if Ra'ūf didn't survive the childbirth? What if I lost her, too?

These thoughts disturbed my peace of mind so much and carried me away with them to such an extent that when I came back to my normal state of mind, I had already put the last of the town's houses behind me and was well into the periphery of the desert. A cool breeze rushed across my face from the direction of the wilderness, and the question occurred to me as to why I had come out here in the first place. A child who was destined to become the slave of a non-Shī'a owner would be better off dead. I was overwhelmed by a strong feeling of dislike for myself. What kind of person have they chosen to represent them, I thought. I envisaged the terrified eyes of the children, the wailing of the womenfolk, and the pitiful remorse in the looks of the men. When a whole nation of people is to be annihilated, what possible difference could it make whether Ra'ūf or my child survived or died in childbirth? Let them die. Surely, that would be better than their falling into a lifetime of slavery.

    I took off my robe and turban and then took off my shoes and flung them in some direction out of my way, then I ran into the heart of the wilderness, cursing myself for clutching onto the passing pleasures of this pitiable realm of existence, the *dunyā*.[14]

    I tripped on something and fell down. I straightened myself up and sat upright and reprimanded myself: Have you forgotten that evil conspiracy of the sultan and vizier, and the fate of the people which is in your hands? Have you forgotten your duty before them?

---

[14] What is known as the lower world in the Qur'ānic cosmology.

Are you thinking of nothing but the fate of your wife and unborn child, heedless of the fate of everyone else's families?

I struck myself on the head with my hands. I felt so ashamed that I wanted the Earth to open up its mouth and swallow me whole. I grabbed two fistfuls of sand and threw them on my own head, and asked God to help me forget about what was happening in my own household and to liberate my heart from anything and everything that had to do with *this* world; to free my heart of the love of anything other than Himself, so that I could call upon the Imam and supplicate to him with a love that is worthy of him.

I then sat down and stared into the heart of the wilderness, into the heart of a darkness that was gradually becoming lightened by the light of a rising moon. But no matter how I tried to forget my thoughts of those two beings who were so dear to my heart, I could not do so; and it seemed that the more I tried, the faster they clung to the corners of my mind, and Ra'ūf's darkened face would appear with greater clarity and resolution before my eyes. The thought of her being taken into slavery sent shivers up and down my spine. I cried out, 'Forgive me, O Imam, I have come to seek your help; but as you can see, my heart and mind are with my family and are heedless of you.'

The Mystery of the Miraculous Pomegranate

I supplicated to God ﷻ, 'O Munificent Lord, have mercy on me! Allow me to forget those who are dearest to me, so that the thought of one who is dearer than they are can enter my heart.' I prostrated myself and wept so much that I had difficulty breathing for a while. I called His Eminence the Ḥujjah[15] ﷺ first in my heart, and then I vocalised his blessed name with my mouth. I repeated his name so many times that it became a shout from the bottom of my lungs. I was out of breath and had damaged my vocal cords, but it suddenly seemed as if the entirety of my being was filled with my love for him, and at the same time had been emptied of love for anything else, [other than God ﷻ, of course, for Whom he was the divinely-appointed representative].

I rose up and started to walk, while I still wept in my desperate state of supplicatory exigence. The thorns of the thorn bushes pierced and tore up my feet, and the chill night air of the desert made me shiver. As tears rolled down my cheeks, I complained, 'If you do not help me, if you do not respond to my pleas for help, I will kill myself. I will not go back. O hope and light of

---

[15] *Ḥujjah*: one of the titles of the Twelfth Imam ﷺ. Professor Hāmid Algar provides the following definition: "The designation *Ḥujjah* ("proof") given to the Imams has a twofold sense. First, through the qualities they manifest, they are proofs of the existence of God ﷻ and of the veracity of the religion He has revealed, [and serve the function of acting as exemplary models of ethical conduct to be emulated]. Second, [by serving this function and providing such an example,] they constitute proofs [= evidence] to be advanced on the Day of Judgment against those who claim they were uninformed of God's ﷻ law [and intended dispensational order]."

the world, O you who came to my aid for such a paltry need; how then could you not come to our aid for such a great need as we have now?'

My feet were bleeding, my voice box didn't work anymore, and my body had become numb from the cold, but my weeping continued nonstop, and there was a veritable storm raging in my heart. I had stopped my pleas and supplications. I just wanted to see him and didn't want anything else. My heartbeat with a passion for nothing but that. I loved him and just wanted to see him, just for the sake of seeing him; not in order to ask him for something, but just to see him so that I could then die at his feet in peace. At that moment, my heart desired nothing but being in his presence.

The night was coming to an end, and my power was waning. I no longer had the power to leave, nor did I have the power or ability to continue calling out to him. I fell on my knees facing the horizon where the light of dawn was breaking and said to myself, 'The night passed, and he didn't appear.'

In my heart of hearts, I was neither resentful nor hopeless. My passion and love for the Imam ﷺ had not diminished even an iota. I said, 'Let our bodies and our souls, our very beings, be sacrificed for your cause. In your wisdom, you must have seen the greater good in not appearing before me, my dear Mahdī.[16] In

---

[16] Yet another, more popular title for the Twelfth Imam ﷺ. The Mahdi also has a dual meaning: the Guided One, and the Guide or Guiding One.

your wisdom, you must have determined our capacities, merit, and competence to be at this level. Our faith must have major flaws and must not be worthy of such an intercession by you. So please forgive us for all of our weaknesses. Please forgive us... Please forgive us...'

I asked his forgiveness so many times that I tired myself out and couldn't say it anymore. I prostrated myself and wept at our own sorry state and the state we would be in the hereafter. I was numb all over from the cold. I might have passed out at any moment. I suddenly felt a warmth behind me. I thought the sun had come up, but then quickly realised that the sun was before me and not behind me. I felt the strange presence of a person behind me. I thought it was some sort of delusion, but then I felt the weight of his hand on my right shoulder. I gathered my senses and raised my head, and saw a tall, broad-shouldered man who was standing behind me, looking at me. I had never seen a pair of eyes that shone so brightly in my whole life. I stood up and cleaned my tears from my face with the backs of my hands. His clothes were similar to those worn by the seminary students in Persia and his robe was undulating in the breeze. His black turban set off his white *'abā'* (body-length robe) beautifully, and he had a very handsome, luminous face.

'My God ﷺ! What a ruckus you raised!' he said.
'Who are you?' I asked.
'A Muslim,' he said,
'Are you Shia?' I asked.

'I am,' he said.

'Well, I had a great need, for which I was beseeching our occulted Imam ﷺ for help. I called out all night to him, but he didn't come,' I explained, at the tail end of which a lump formed in my throat, causing my voice to break.

He replied with a penetrating voice, 'If you knew him, you would know that there could never be a plaintiff who asked for his help from the bottom of his heart and have his plea go unanswered.'

I struck myself on my head with both hands and said, 'Of course! You are right. Woe to me for not being worthy. I have desired the paltry, unworthy pleasures of this world, and have neglected [the values of] my Master.'

Then he came forward, wiped my tears with the tip of his fingers, and said, 'I would not be an Imam, so help me God ﷻ, if I were to hear such heartfelt pleas for help and not respond to them. Look into my eyes, Muḥammad the son of 'Īsā! The jasmine flower that you asked me for, your Fāṭimah, is now sleeping soundly in her mother's arms.'

There they were: his luminous oval face, his black beard, his long, drawn-out brows that were slightly touching in the middle, and those mild green penetrating eyes! I shouted, 'You came! You responded to a wretch such as myself!' I fell to my knees and kissed his blessed feet.

He hastened to raise me back up and said, 'Be calm, and listen to what I tell you.'

I said, 'Are you aware of the conspiracy that is afoot?'

He said, 'Yes, I know. Now pay attention, Muḥammad! That pomegranate is not a natural phenomenon, but is the handiwork of the vizier.'

Astonished, I asked, 'But how is that possible?'

The Imam took a step back and stared into the distance. His face glowed with the sacred light that emanated from him. He said, 'There is a pomegranate tree in the vizier's garden. He made a spherical mould inside of which the words that were inscribed on the pomegranate were embossed. This spherical mould was then placed around a small pomegranate and secured firmly on it, ensuring that the embossed sentence would be inscribed on the pomegranate when it grew into the mould.'

I was grinding my teeth together without realising it. I shook my head and said, 'Curse the vizier and his diabolical conspiracy, by means of which he wanted to kill thousands of people. But then how are we to counter his plot?'

The Imam said, 'Know, O Muḥammad, that I am fully aware of everything that has befallen your community, and of every act of persecution that our enemies have committed against you. And know that I will not forget you, for otherwise our enemies would destroy you. Now, I'll teach you what needs to be done, after which you will go back to your people and do as I bid you to do.'

The Mystery of the Miraculous Pomegranate

And so it was that I walked shoulder to shoulder with the Imam, and it was my lot to hear his alluring voice, smell his heavenly scent, and feel completely at peace despite the cold of the desert, my torn-up feet, and the evil machinations of our enemies.

We reached the outlying dwellings of our town. I heard the buzz of people talking at a distance. It was time for me to bid farewell to the Imam. I took his blessed hand and bowed down and kissed it.

I said, 'I am in your debt.'

He said, 'The greater your righteousness and the better your moral conduct, the closer and stronger our bond becomes. Now go back to your people, kiss your little Fāṭimah's forehead for me, and ask Sheikh Dhākir to pronounce the call to prayer (*adhān*) in her ear in the name of my mother, [Lady] Fāṭimah^t uz-Zahrā (the Luminous) [ﷺ].' Suddenly, something went through my mind, but before I could vocalise it, the Imam said, 'Sheikh Dhākir has such a high station in terms of the rightfulness of his mode of conduct and his piety that if he had called upon me in his house, I would have appeared to him there. But he became an instrument by means of which your faith and *taqwā*[17] were tested.'

---

[17] *Taqwā*: a righteousness and pious devotion of the soul and of one's character which is informed by a fear of the possible everlasting consequences of appearing before God ﷻ on the Day of Judgement and the possibility of the failure to perform well before one's Lord of Providence and Cherisher (*rabb*) in this ultimate, fateful Judgement.

I couldn't stop looking at him and didn't want to depart from his presence. Suddenly, some of the womenfolk who were waiting started to shout out. I turned around to see where the noise was coming from and saw that they had spotted me. I turned back to say a final farewell to the Imam, but he was gone. I ran forward so that I might perhaps see him again, or even see his footprint, but he was nowhere to be found, nor was there any trace of his footprints.

Our group consisted of the same notables who had been invited to the sultan's palace four days earlier. Occasionally, one of my comrades would place a hand on my shoulder or kiss my forehead out of excitement, pride, and by way of thanksgiving and gratitude. Our shoulders had slouched so much during these past three days and nights that we had taken on their form as a habit. But now we held our shoulders up high, and our eyes sparkled with confidence. This could especially be seen in Sheikh Dhākir's eyes, who held my arm and repeated several times that my faith was a great source of our dignity and pride.

When we got to the sultan's palace, we saw that his sentinels acted towards us as if they had already sharpened their scimitars for our beheadings. When we entered the palace's entryway, the vizier opened his arms and said, 'Ah, they have arrived. Our lambs have come to the slaughterhouse on their own feet!'

I felt at peace in my heart at the fate that was to befall the vizier. The sultan said, 'Your three-day reprieve is over. Now tell me which path you have opted to take.'

I raised my hand and said, 'We shall refute the so-called "proof" of the pomegranate with irrefutable evidence and substantiations.' When I said this, I saw the vizier's eyes visibly widen in surprise and saw that a shiver ran through his body.

The sultan said, 'Well, we are waiting.'

I said, 'We will only prove the falsity of this so-called "proof" in the vizier's house!'

The vizier shouted, 'What kind of nonsense is this that you have concocted! What does the refutation of such a clear proof have to do with my house and the sanctity of the privacy of my family?'

Sheikh Dhākir said, 'Hold your tongue and respect your own honour and self-respect. If the sultan is just, our request will pose no problems for his ruling; and if you have no doubt about the natural nature of the creation of the pomegranate, then you will have nothing to fear either.'

The vizier held his head up high and said, 'I have no doubt, nor do I have any fear!'

The sultan said as he stood up, 'If you can prove the true nature of this pomegranate, I am willing to come to the end of the world with you to see it!'

The Mystery of the Miraculous Pomegranate

The vizier moved fast and had positioned himself ahead of us. The words of the Imam reverberated in my ears: 'Don't let the vizier get ahead of you and enter his house before you do!'

To put an end to this state of affairs, I said in a loud voice, 'The vizier is in such a hurry that he has forgotten to maintain the protocol of the dignity of the sultan and proceeds before him!'

The sultan frowned. As the vizier slowed and took his place behind the sultan, he said, 'Far be it from me to have the temerity to do such a thing! My intention was to act as an escort, or else I wouldn't have...' His voice trailed off, and he stood behind the sultan. I glanced over at Sheikh Dhākir, who gave me a smile and a nod of appreciation.

We entered the vizier's house. Just to the right of the entryway, there was a flight of stairs that reached up to a room on the second floor, just as the Imam had taught me. I said, 'We will reveal the mystery of the pomegranate in *that* room up there.'

The vizier yelled out again, 'You will do no such thing! My house is not a free-for-all, you know, for you to be able to come and go anywhere you please and invade the privacy of my household. After all, it is not as if *I* have made that pomegranate. What warrant do you have to search my house!?' He was seething with indignation.

I said, 'You know full well who has made that pomegranate, for why else would you make such a fuss?'

The vizier stepped lively and said, 'My concern, or 'fuss' as you put it, has to do with outsiders (*nāmaḥram*[18]) who want to feast their unwelcome, spying little eyes on the honour of my family (*nāmūs*[19])!'

The sultan said, 'The vizier is right. What kind of ruse is this that you are playing at?'

Sheikh Dhākir replied, 'Upon my word of honour, sire, you will not find a single woman in that room.'

The vizier shouted, 'Yes, there is!! Who knows better, me or you?'

I said, 'Allow me to enter the room. If there is any woman in that room, I swear that I will accept any ruling that the sultan rules against me; whatever it is, be it the taking of my life, the forfeiture of my property, or anything else.'

---

[18] *Maḥram* is a category of people in the sacred law of Islam (the *sharī'a*) who are related to each other by blood or marriage such that they are not allowed to marry one another. For example, a mother and son, or a father and daughter or daughter in law, or brothers and sisters. Because there is such a close familial bond between them that no sexual intercourse can ever take place between them. The females within the *maḥram* circle are not obligated to veil their hair with a scarf when they are in the company of males (such as their father or brothers) within their *maḥram* circle and not in public. *Maḥram* is contrasted with *nāmaḥram*, which is a category of people who are strangers and whose gaze, therefore, is not licit according to the sacred law of God ﷻ. Men must lower their gaze when in the company of *nāmaḥram* women.

[19] *Nāmūs*: the order, honour, self-respect and dignity of oneself and one's wards and household.

The Mystery of the Miraculous Pomegranate

The sultan said, 'What he says makes sense. Let him enter, O vizier. This is in our favour!'

I wanted to climb the stairs, but the vizier rushed forward and blocked my path. I said, 'Do you refuse the order of the sultan?'

But despite this, he ran up to the room. The Imam had stressed the point that I mustn't let the vizier enter the room before me, so I ran up after him and just as he reached the door, I grabbed him by the scruff of his neck, pulled him back, and entered the room first. There was a little shelf on the wall to the right of the room on which there was a white sack, just as the Imam ﷺ had said there would be. I ran forward and grabbed it before the vizier had a chance to take it. He was considerably shorter than I was, and as he was struggling to take the sack away from me, the vizier shouted, 'You heathen! You thief! How dare you steal my belongings in front of my very eyes in my own house?!'

The sultan and my comrades had entered the room by then. The sultan said to the vizier, 'Stop your nonsense.' And then he turned to me and said, 'And you! What kind of antics are you playing at?'

I opened the knot of the sack and took out the spherical mould that had been used on the pomegranate and raised it up high for all to see. My comrades all praised God ﷻ in gratitude. The sultan, whose eyes had popped out of their sockets in astonishment, leaned against a wall. I gave the mould to the sultan and said, 'There is a pomegranate tree in

The Mystery of the Miraculous Pomegranate

your vizier's garden. He made this mould with baked clay, and as you can see, he has embossed the same lettering that appears inscribed on the pomegranate inside the mould. He secured this mould around a small pomegranate, and when the pomegranate grew larger, it grew around the embossed lettering, causing the words to be inscribed on the pomegranate's peel in a way that appeared to be nature's handiwork, rather than the diabolical work of the vizier.'

The sultan was speechless. The vizier came forward and said, 'This is a lie! He is exaggerating!!'

The sultan shouted, 'Shut up, you fool! You deceived me too!!'

The vizier drew back. He had gone as pale as a ghost. I said, 'This was the vizier's false "proof" in his refutation of the Shī'a faith. Now, with God's ﷻ leave, and if Your Honour permits me, I will provide you with a true reason and proof in affirmation of the veracity of our faith using that same pomegranate.'

The sultan took a kerchief out of his pocket, wiped the sweat of his brow, then said, 'Tell me what your proof is. I very much doubt that it will be as strange as the mystery that you have just revealed.'

I said, 'Oh, but it is, sire. May I have the pomegranate? I will open it before your eyes, and you will see fire and smoke and hot ash come out of it!'

The pomegranate was back at the sultan's palace, so we made our way back there, and he ordered it to be brought and given to me. Just as I was about to take it from the sultan's hands, the vizier rushed forward, grabbed the pomegranate, and yelled, 'You have made fools of yourselves! You will now see that nothing will come out of this pomegranate but pomegranate seeds. As he said this, he broke the pomegranate open. Suddenly, black smoke and hot ash gushed out onto the vizier's face. He held his face in his hands and yelled, 'Aaaah... I'm on fire! It's burning me!!'

All of his beard and hair had fizzled up in flames. The sultan said, 'Take this fraud away from my sight and kill him!'

The vizier had started to plead and beg for mercy, but they removed him by force. The sultan stood up and came forward. He embraced me and said, 'What you did today was beyond the means of any ordinary human being. Tell me, who gave you this knowledge that you had?'

I replied, 'Last night, our occulted Imam, His Eminence the Ḥujjah ﷺ, paid me a visit. It was he who revealed these secrets to me.'

The sultan went to Sheikh Dhākir, took hold of his hand, and managed to kiss it despite the sheikh's protestations. He then said, 'Forgive me! I swear upon the honour of your Imam, I was lost, but now I am found. From this point forward, I too will be a devotee and sincere partisan (*shī'a*) of my Master, Imam Ali ﷺ, and of the other Shī'a Imams ﷺ, and I will have a special place in my heart for the Twelfth Imam, the Lord of the Age ﷺ. Will you be so kind, O sheikh, to teach me the principles of your creed?'

Sheikh Dhākir said, 'May God ﷻ be praised for ridding us of the evil of the vizier, and for joining Your Honour to our ranks so that you can add to the dissemination of the just and true Shī'a faith.'

Then the sultan repeated the names of the Twelve Imams ﷺ and testified to their divinely sanctioned guardianship-type sovereignty and authority (*wilāyah* [20]).

---

[20] *Wilāyah* is a multifaceted term which defies translation; its range of meaning includes, at a minimum, the following

different facets: 1. Closeness or proximity, 2. contiguity, 3. spiritual affinity, 4. religious uniformity, cohesion and integrality, 5. social inter-connectivity and inter-dependence based on shared creedal beliefs; 6. dominion, 7. sovereignty, 8. proxy sovereignty or regency, 9. guardianship, 10. governance, 11. jurisdiction, 12. reign, 13. command, 14. custodianship, 15. authority, and 16. religious uniformity and the feeling of inter-dependence and solidarity which obtains as a result of that uniformity, harmony, cohesion, integrality and unicity of purpose. *Wilāyah* means propinquity (spiritual proximity) to God ﷻ, but in most Shi'a contexts also refers to the regency or guardianship-type sovereign authority which is vested in the Fourteen Immaculates as a result of that proximity. *Wilāyah* refers to a special type of sovereignty that is the central pillar of the Shī'a conception of the imāmate or the Islamic vision of the way in which the polity of the community is to be structured, with the *imām* or leader of the community having *walīyic* or guardianship-type sovereignty over his adherents, and to whom a pledge of allegiance is due and which affirms the Imams' regency over the affairs of the community; i.e. guardianship-type authority to govern over those who have attained to faith in the divinely-sanctioned social order.

The Mystery of the Miraculous Pomegranate

8

I accompanied Sheikh Dhākir back to his house, and not a single word was exchanged between us on the way there. He was holding onto my arm. A strange calm had come over his face, and his eyes sparkled. I said, 'I doubt I will be up to the task.'

He bent down, kissed my forehead, and said, 'Who could be worthier than you? You are a scholar, have a strong writing style, and most important of all, were the immediate beneficiary of this great act of grace.'

I said, 'I will do my best to write the tale as it ought to be written...'

He took my hands in his and said, 'Write about the feelings, the emotions, and the atmosphere, and every moment that you experienced, from the very first day up until now. Let everyone who reads the tale realise who the true believers are.'

I told him, 'His Eminence the Qā'im [21] ﷺ said, "Sheikh Dhākir is a true believer, for he can see me at any time merely by asking to see me." So why was there such a need for you to send a lowly man such as myself into the wilderness?'

He got his emotions under control and said, 'I will never forget the trouble that you went through, especially as I myself did nothing. Nor could I have done anything, because this incident was a divine test to gauge the measure of your faith.'

I said, 'Praise God ﷻ for allowing me to undergo the test without being a source of shame to our community.'

He brought my head forward, kissed my forehead, and said, 'May your reward be with that same God ﷻ who heeded our call for help.'

I bid him farewell and headed back home. The sky was overcast, but the sun's rays made their way down to Earth through an opening in the clouds. The air smelled like it was about to rain. When I got home, before I could knock on the door, I heard Fāṭimah crying, and her cries were inviting me to smell the scent of her jasmine fragrance.

---

[21] This is another title of the Master of the Age ﷺ, which means, 'He who will rise up [to establish God's ﷻ order on Earth]'.

www.ingramcontent.com/pod-product-compliance
Lightning Source LLC
Chambersburg PA
CBHW030327080526
44584CB00012B/750